Travels of the Heart
Developing Your Inner Leader

Bobbi Kahler

Travels of the Heart: Developing Your Inner Leader
© 2010 Bobbi Kahler, Six Seconds | All Rights Reserved

Cover Design by Brett Casey; Book Design by Joshua Freedman

ISBN: 978-1-935667-01-8
Library of Congress Control Number: 2010923690
Printed and bound in the USA

Six Seconds Press
San Francisco, CA
www.6seconds.org/tools

Acknowledgements

To Rick, for always asking "why not?"

As you will read in these pages, there have been many people who have contributed to my travels. Some relationships were fleeting; some will last a lifetime. Some stood in the darkness of doubt with me. Most stood in the moment of possibility. They all helped me to learn a little more about myself. They all revealed a little more of the picture. I am deeply grateful for their support, friendship and wisdom.

Introduction

When I was twenty-two, I was already on my seventh job. I was always a star performer. The problem was that my star kept burning out.

I would burn intensely and brightly and lift others around me – for a short period of time. Then I would become restless and frustrated and impatient with my teammates. I was considering switching jobs again and I was considering my bad luck: why was it that no matter what job I had, people who made my life miserable always surrounded me? I was enjoying the self-congratulation of blaming everyone else, but then something happened. I was hit by this realization: The common denominator across all seven of those jobs was me. Could it be that the problem wasn't with everybody else? Maybe the problem was within me. I have to admit that this wasn't nearly as much fun as blaming everyone else! But it was more powerful. It began to sow the seeds for my journey to becoming a leader.

In the course of that journey, I learned that blaming doesn't work, nor, at the other end, does dreaming that others will rescue us;

instead we need to take ownership of our own power, be our own heroes and our own rescuers. Each of us has a vast reservoir of personal power inside. If we don't use it, we simply drift along on other people's currents. But if we do, we create the future.

It is our job – and our responsibility, and our gift – to tap into that power. Then, if we want to become leaders, we can share that power with others. Put another way, we have to lead ourselves before we can lead others.

The process of learning to use my own power has been both exciting and scary. It has not always been a smooth journey, and I don't think there's a perfect path that everyone can follow. So instead I'd like to share a series of snapshots from my travels toward leadership.

Each snapshot begins with a reflection, many from the journals I've kept over my lifetime. Then, I offer some reflection questions for your own journal writing. The snapshots are not sequential – they're a collection of the most important lessons that have helped me. Some will be ideal for you today, some you might want to save for another time. The book is divided into three sections, which roughly follow my experience of learning to lead:

One. Becoming Aware – this will help you learn more about yourself and what drives you.

Two. Making Choices – awareness is essential – but how do you act on that? Knowing isn't enough, action is required.

Three. Tapping Into Our Power – now that you've figured out what's driving you and how to make better choices, it's time to decide where to go! How will you use your power?

This is a book to read, but even more, it's a book to do. As you'll read in a few pages, reflection is one of our most valuable tools for growth. So I urge you to give yourself the gift of learning – a gift you can unwrap by writing in your journal using the questions and prompts in each snapshot.

This book is designed to be a self-learning tool. It is a way for you to gain insight into your behaviors, action, choices and consequences. It is never intended to be judgmental. As you'll read, there are many things that, given the opportunity, I would have done differently. I imagine the same is true for all of us. We can look at these mistakes as disasters, but I'd rather we each find solace in recognizing our mistakes as a way we've gained the wisdom to choose and do differently. Our lives provide a rich learning environment. This book is intended to help you harvest that wisdom.

Section One: Becoming Aware

Notes from My Journal

When I was in my early twenties, I always felt blindsided by emotions. Blindsided and ruled by my emotions, I should say. It wasn't pleasant. It felt as though someone else was in control of my life and my emotional state. As a result, I was often angry, resentful and not very hopeful. I made very poor choices.

I did an exercise once where I looked back at the different chapters of my life and named them. When I looked back at the year that I turned 23, I instantly knew the title of that year: The Year I Lived the Country Music Song. That was the year that I got divorced, my grandmother died, I had a massive fight with a sister (potentially ending the relationship forever), I lost my best friend, and I was so broke that I was working two jobs (both at 40 hours per week) and barely keeping my head above water. I love country music, but I prefer listening to it than living it!

I will never forget that New Year's Eve. I worked my two jobs and I got home just a little after midnight – if you can call an empty apartment home. I sat there in the darkness, pondering the course of my life so far. I was mad. It wasn't turning out the way that I thought it should. I was a good student in high school. Yet, here I sat, working two jobs, with no college education. My parents didn't believe in college. They believed that when you turn eighteen, you move out and you take care of yourself. So far, I wasn't doing a very good job of it. In the darkness of that moment, I began searching for someone to blame. There had to be someone who had done this to me! In a painful flash of insight, I identified the villain: me. ***In that split second, I realized that my life was a reflection of the choices that I had made***

so far. I have to confess, it wasn't the villain I was hoping to find! But, while that was discouraging, another thought occurred to me: if my life was a reflection of the choices that I had made so far, then, if I could learn how to make better choices – and develop the discipline to follow those choices – couldn't I get a better result? The result I wanted?

I could no longer hide from the truth. On that cold, blustery, dark New Year's Eve night some twenty years ago, I took responsibility for myself and my future and began my journey. It began by learning about myself and coming to understand myself. It wasn't always pleasant. I had some very unpleasant – if not downright ugly – things to confront about myself. I was willing to confront those things if, by doing so, I could uncover the potential I knew I had and the person I knew I could be.

For Your Journal:

- *This poses the critical question: Who do you want to be?*

- *What is your ideal image of yourself?*

- *What results are you getting right now that you like? That you don't like?*

- *What choices of yours are creating those results?*

Our Stories

"Never let someone tell you what you can or cannot do."

Kathy Kahler (my mother)

As a child, I had severe speech problems that lingered into my teens. Despite a dismal diagnosis from the speech pathologist, my mother wouldn't let me believe that the problems were insurmountable. To her, it was simply a problem that, with enough hard work and perseverance, I could overcome. This became one of my core stories about myself: that if I simply set my mind to something, I could do it.

Core stories are those things that we believe about ourselves. Each of us, over time, develops core stories about ourselves. Often other people script our core stories for us (parents, siblings, teachers). Sometimes these have valuable truth, and sometimes these hold us back.

My "you can do what you put your mind to" story has been a source of power for me. On the other hand, some core stories have the opposite effect and they diminish our power. It's important that we identify those negative core stories so that we can challenge them and begin to rewrite them. It's also important for us to identify our positive core stories so we can tap into the fuel they provide. **As with any other type of story writing, sometimes stories about ourselves are true, and sometimes they are fiction.** Do you know which is which for you?

For Your Journal

- *What is one of your core stories that diminishes your power?*

- *How did you learn that story?*

- *What parts of that story are true? (Perhaps it was true at one point, but few of us are exactly the same person today as we were when we were thirteen.)*

- *What are your most positive and powerful core stories?*

- *How did you learn these stories?*

- *How have they helped you in the past? How do they help you today? (Do they give you hope, courage, strength?)*

> **Action**
>
> The next time you find yourself thinking or replaying one of the negative stories, challenge it! You have other stories that are more powerful.

The Wisdom of Failure

*"You did what you knew how to do,
and when you knew better, you did better."*

Maya Angelou

I really dislike making mistakes. When I was younger, it was an acute phobia. Since I don't believe that there is an official term for this phobia, I will call it "errorphobia" (which does show up in Internet searches!). Errorphobia, as most phobias do, truly limited my life. I would only take action when I saw a high probability of success. If I did make a mistake, I made excuses for it. I became so proficient at excuse-making that my mother suggested that perhaps a career in politics was in my future.

I knew when I made a mistake, even if I couldn't admit it out loud. But a strange thing happened: The less I admitted my mistakes, the more that I obsessed about them! When we hold on to our mistakes, we are really holding on to judging ourselves harshly. Is there really any value in that? What do we gain by being our own worst critic? Maybe it was a way to make sure no one else could criticize me.

One day when I was in my mid-twenties, I was driving to work and I saw a sign outside of a church that said, "Admitting a mistake is just another way of saying that you are wiser today than you were yesterday."

This simple statement completely changed the way that I

looked at my mistakes. Instead of something scary and terrible, I decided to consider mistakes as badges of wisdom. What had I learned? What would I do differently in the future?

For Your Journal

- *When you make a mistake, how do you respond? Do you deny it (to yourself or others)? Do you bounce back quickly or get paralyzed by it?*

- *Do you judge yourself?*

- *If you could see the mistake as a badge of wisdom, how could that help you?*

- *What are some questions you could ask yourself to help you see that wisdom?*

I Shouldn't Feel...

"He who lacks time to mourn lacks time to mend."

William Shakespeare

My little sister is going through a lot of changes right now. Her husband, a manager at GM, has been relocated from Oklahoma City to St. Louis. In Oklahoma, they have a house in the country with plenty of room for their kids to play. They have a trampoline, a swimming pool, and their neighbors own horses which the kids get to ride. My niece, age 6, has already saved up half the money she needs to buy her own horse, which they have room for in Oklahoma but which remains to be seen once they move. My sister knows how hard the move is on the kids and she feels sad about it. To complicate things, my sister has had a dog since 1989, and now the dog is sick, and they have to consider if it's time to put the dog to rest.

I was talking with my sister yesterday and she started crying. She quickly apologized for being a baby and said that she knows that her problems aren't that bad, that there are plenty of people out there who have serious problems. It struck me that so many of us do what she did: we discount our feelings. She has every reason to feel sad and to feel the stress of moving and how it affects her kids.

Many of us do that – we deny some or our feelings. "I shouldn't feel sad…," or, "I should feel lucky that…" or "there's no reason to be so angry…" or even, "I know it's silly to be so happy when…."

When we deny the feeling, we're judging ourselves, saying we're weak or bad for having the feeling. But that makes it impossible to listen to and learn from the feeling. What if the feeling has valuable wisdom? Next time try just naming the feeling and saying to yourself, "That's interesting, I wonder why I'm feeling that?"

For Your Journal:

- *When have you denied or rejected your own feelings?*
- *How were you judging yourself by doing that?*
- *How did that affect you?*
- *If you had acknowledged the feeling, how might it have helped you?*

Reflection

"Reading without reflecting is like eating without digesting."

Edmund Burke

I was at a coffee shop recently. I was sitting at a table, enjoying my coffee and thinking; not reading, not writing, not listening to my iPod, just thinking.

The person at the next table leaned over and asked what I was doing. I replied that I was thinking. She looked a bit horrified and then said, "Oh, I don't like a lot of quiet time; I like the distractions of noise. Thinking can be scary."

I thought about what she'd said. Sometimes it is daunting to be still and to be quiet and to just be alone with your thoughts. I remember a class I took in college where we were discussing being a life-long learner. My professor stated it this way: without reflection, we don't grow.

When you're busy doing, there are constant distractions taking you one direction or another. Stimulus can give you energy and maybe provoke new questions. However, **the quiet is where you find the answers.**

Becoming Aware | 11

For Your Journal

- *Do you make time in your day that is clear of distractions and noise so that you can reflect on the events of the day? If not, try it for one month. You'll be surprised at what you discover.*

- *Try asking these questions (and you don't have to answer all of these every day!):*

    - *What good results did I get today?*
    - *How did I contribute to those results?*
    - *How can I duplicate those results?*
    - *What did I do great today?*
    - *Who did I help today?*
    - *How did I live my values today?*
    - *Was I disappointed today? By whom or what?*
    - *Did I contribute to that outcome? If so, how?*

Changing Expectations

"We are always paid for our suspicion by finding what we suspect."

Henry David Thoreau

I was talking with one of my friends recently and she told me that she was dreading an upcoming family reunion because she and her siblings always fight when they get together. Always. As she talked, I could tell that not only do they fight when they are together but she was already thinking of things to fight about! I gently pointed this out to her and asked her if she ever thought that contributed to the outcome. She sheepishly laughed and admitted that her way of thinking did actually increase her anger.

How many times do you hear someone say one of the following?

- *I don't like the way my mother-in-law treats me, but I guess that's just the way it is.*
- *My brother and I can't be in the same room without fighting.*
- *My boss never listens to what I have to say.*
- *Selling is a confrontational undertaking.*
- *Drivers in this city are nasty.*

Becoming Aware

They each have a long history of experience to support their claim, and they are good at proving themselves right. They hold onto the expectation, and then create that result (even though they say they don't want it to happen!).

The first step to changing the outcome of a situation or experience is to change our expectation. If I expect drivers to be nasty, I will notice every nasty driver; however, if I expect that drivers are courteous, I will see plenty of courteous drivers. Not that there won't be any nasty drivers, but I find that when I am expecting courteous drivers, I am not as frustrated by the nasty ones; I figure that they are just having a bad day.

The first step in changing the outcome of a recurring pattern is to change your expectations.

> **Action**
>
> Pick one outcome that dissatisfies you (maybe start with something small) and picture a new and desirable outcome. Go into that experience expecting the desirable outcome. You may be surprised. At the very least, you won't arrive angry!

For Your Journal:

- *What are some negative expectations that you hold about others?*

- *How does holding those expectations affect you?*

  (For example, if you expect a person to be confrontational, do you find yourself tensing up before the meeting?)

- *How does your expectation affect the outcome?*

  (Using the above example, if you tense up before the meeting, do you think the other person picks up on that? They almost certainly do no matter how hard you may try to hide it. Does your anxiety cause you to possibly misread what they are saying? Does your communication skill diminish as a result of your anxiety?)

- *If your negative expectation is about someone, brainstorm some possible empathetic explanations for their behavior. In other words, what concerns, worries, fears, etc., might they be experiencing that lead them to act the way they do?*

Becoming Aware

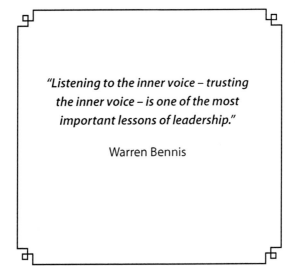

"Listening to the inner voice – trusting the inner voice – is one of the most important lessons of leadership."

Warren Bennis

There's Nothing I Can Do

"Why do you have to have any struggle in your life?"

Thomas Leonard

Many of us have resigned ourselves to the fact that we are going to have areas in our lives where there will be struggle. There are things that we are just going to have to tolerate: the way a co-worker treats us or the way our mother treats us or the way a client treats us. You can supply your own list. While maybe it's easier to accept that, there's a major problem with this thinking: **By resigning ourselves to tolerating those things we don't like, we give up any chance of solving the problem.**

I once worked with a woman, Susan, who had a friend, Beth. Beth was a nice woman who smothered Susan with "help." Unfortunately, it wasn't the help that Susan wanted. At one point, Susan said to me, "It drives me crazy! She's not helping me and it frustrates me. But, I guess I just have to accept it." I asked Susan what sort of help she wanted. Once she told me, I asked her, "Why don't you tell Beth this?" Susan replied that she didn't want to hurt Beth's feelings because she knew she was only trying to be helpful. How many of us have said something similar?

Here's the important re-framing of this situation: if Beth (in this example) is truly wanting to be helpful and her motivation is pure, then wouldn't Beth want to know what is really helpful for Susan, and if her motivation isn't pure, isn't it better to know that and move on? I asked Susan to try it and I suggested this language: "You know, Beth, I love that you are so helpful. What would really be the most helpful for me is..." It worked: Beth got to help Susan and Susan got the help she wanted – and she got rid of an annoying frustration.

We all have situations where we've given up. Maybe that's right, and it's not worth putting energy into a solution. On the other hand, maybe we just resign ourselves and tolerate the situation without even trying to solve it.

For Your Journal:

- *What are you tolerating? List at least five situations where you've resigned yourself and given up on solving the problem.*

- *What if you didn't have to just accept the situation – how would it help you to change it?*

- *For each item on your list, what would you like instead? What kind of help do you want (as in Susan's example)?*

- *What is one new way you could ask for what you want rather than tolerating something you don't want?*

Defining Yourself

"Limitations, like fears, are often illusions."

Michael Jordan

I had been a runner for about ten years. At my best, I was up to eight miles, every other day. I could run the eight miles in under an hour. In 2003, I got very sick and it didn't look like I'd ever have a full recovery. At that time, the doctors advised me that my running days were over for good. They offered that I could hope for good days where I could take some short walks.

I worked to regain my health and, in June of 2006, I got to the point where I consistently felt pretty good. It was a massive improvement. As I was out for my walks, I noticed the runners as they passed me and I would think longingly of when I was a runner and I would think to myself, "I used to be a runner. I used to be an athlete." I missed that part of myself; in fact, I felt like a piece of me was missing, but I "knew" that I couldn't run.

After living with that loss – and longing – for a month, I decided that at least I could test to find out if that limitation was still true. When I first got sick it was definitely true, but was it still? If I started running and got sick, then I'd have my answer.

I laced up my shoes, set a reasonable goal for myself (a mile) and headed to the track. The first quarter mile felt incredible; the second quarter mile, reminded me, that running was work – hard work;

by the third quarter mile, I was having a hard time remembering what I ever loved about running. At the end of the mile, however, I remembered: that feeling of strength.

I have been running two to three times a week ever since and I'm gradually increasing my distance. I'm once again a runner; no longer defined by an illness. That one thing – how I define and see myself – made all the difference and it has carried over into every area of my life.

Define yourself by what you can do; not by what you can't.

For Your Journal:

- *Do you define yourself by those things that you can't do or by those things that you can do? List some examples.*

- *What limitations, if no longer true and removed from your self-concept, would lift your spirits and energize you?*

- *Is it time to test them? What's the first one to test and how can you challenge it?*

Owning Your Results

> *"The willingness to accept responsibility for one's own life is the source from which self-respect springs."*
>
> Joan Didion

In high school, I competed on the speech and debate team. At the conclusion of the tournament (which was always on a Saturday), our coach, Mr. Jordan, would tell us to take Sunday off and enjoy and celebrate our success. On a Monday following a tournament, we always had a team meeting. Each two-person team would summarize their results from the tournament. The first question that Mr. Jordan would always ask – win or lose – was "What contributed to those results?" At that point, we began dissecting our results and how we ended up with them.

We were never allowed to simply make excuses. Mr. Jordan hated that! One time, one of the debaters, Jim, said, "The judges just don't like me." Mr. Jordan looked at him and said, "You know, I suspect that you are right. So let's talk about why they don't like you." It was a bit painful at first, but it was a very revealing discussion that led to Jim making some pretty big adjustments (and, not surprisingly, he started getting better results).

At the end of the team meeting, Mr. Jordan would wrap up by telling us that he was proud of our effort and our results. He would then gently remind us that no matter how well – or poorly – we had done at the last tournament, there was a new tournament right around the corner and that we all had a clean slate and an equal shot at winning it. What we did last time, simply didn't determine the outcome of the next tournament.

The teams loved Mr. Jordan and they won frequently. Looking back, I see three essential steps that we can all use:

- *Celebrate your success but don't rest on it.*
- *Take ownership of your results. "What contributed to the results you got?"*
- *Prepare for the next opportunity.*

For Your Journal:

- *What is one success you can celebrate?*
- *Do you know why you are getting the results you are getting?*
- *What is one result you want to change – how did you contribute to that?*
- *What's your next opportunity to do something differently so you get better results?*
- *If you lead a team, how can you use Mr. Jordan's three steps with them?*

Holding Onto the Problem

"There came a time when the risk to remain tight in the bud was more painful than the risk it took to blossom."

Anais Nin

Have you ever met people who just seem to love having a problem? This is the person who comes to you – repeatedly – because they want your help in solving a problem. However, no matter what you suggest, they have a million reasons why it would never solve their problem.

A couple of years ago, I was facilitating a small group discussion. There was one member of the group, we'll call her Sally, who asked for the group to help her with a business problem. The group immediately responded and started asking questions to gain an understanding of the situation. Then they moved on to brainstorming and they generated some really good ideas. Sally shot holes into every idea.

I noticed that she seemed energized when she was dismissing suggestions. Eventually I said, "Sally, you seem almost satisfied that none of these ideas would work for you. I have to ask you: Are you more committed to holding on to the problem or to finding a solution?" There was a long pause and finally Sally said, with stunning honestly, "You know, I think I'm more committed to holding on to the problem. If I solve it, I might not be needed anymore." I've heard this belief expressed in different ways a number of times; there are some intangible benefits to holding onto problems.

When we are faced with a problem that just doesn't want to go away, we have to step back and ask ourselves what we gain by having that problem. In *The Way of Transition: Embracing Life's Most Difficult Moments*, William Bridges writes that we never let go of anything important until we have exhausted every possible way of holding on to it. To what are you more committed: the problem or the solution?

For Your Journal:

- *What problems do you hold onto? Look deeply and challenge yourself.*
- *What do you gain by holding on to them? (What's the pay-off for holding on?)*
- *What would it mean to you if you could let them go or solve them?*

Repeating or Practicing?

"To improve is to change; to be perfect is to change often."

Winston Churchill

Most likely, Michael Jordan was a pretty bad basketball player the very first day he picked up a ball. So he didn't become the best basketball player in the world by simply practicing what he knew when he first started. His work ethic and his commitment to practice are legendary and certainly contributed to his success. However, practice doesn't just mean repetition. It means refining what we know and making adjustments based on the experience. Practice means we are developing.

I once was talking to a speaker at a networking event and he told me that he spends hours and hours rehearsing his speech. I asked him how he rehearsed. He told me that he simply says the words of his speech over and over and over again. I asked him if he thought about the words and their meaning and how an audience might respond. He said he didn't because that would get in the way of his memorization.

There's a big difference between memorizing and practicing! He missed the opportunity to make the words better, to make them more relevant to his audience, to make sure that they were the right words.

We all know people who say "I have twenty years of experience," when what they really have is one year of experience repeated twenty times! All of us do this in some ways. We memorize instead of practice. We say, "I've always done it that way." We get really good at doing the wrong thing. But to move toward mastery, we have to be willing to change and grow – and to do it often.

For Your Journal:

- *What are you repeating over and over instead of practicing?*
- *How does it feel to practice versus repeat?*
- *What is one "repeater" that you are ready to let go of and turn into practicing?*
- *How do you challenge your way of doing things?*
- *How do you incorporate new knowledge or insight?*

Action

If you hear yourself say the words, "But, I've always done it that way," you should hear loud warning bells in your head. Confront yourself: Are you repeating or practicing?

Cocky or Confident?

"Confidence comes not from always being right but from not fearing to be wrong."

Peter T. Mcintyre

When I was about 10 years old, we had a magnificent and sudden spring thaw which sent the creek way over its banks. How exciting! I convinced my best friend, Harold, to get closer to the creek to get a better look. I still wasn't satisfied so I sold Harold on the idea that we could build a raft out of some boards and small tree branches and some other random debris. It wasn't easy to convince him, but he eventually agreed. He shouldn't have.

As soon as we had tied the miscellaneous bits together, I pronounced the raft seaworthy (or, at least, creekworthy). We jumped on board and instantly our feet and ankles got wet. I assured him that we wouldn't sink any more; which worked right up until our knees were submerged. At that point, we abandoned ship and swam back to shore.

I have thought about this incident many times and I always come back to the same question: **why did he listen to me?** Perhaps, at 10, Harold hadn't learned the difference between cockiness and confidence.

I was loud and strong in my words, appearing sure (on the outside), but that was cockiness, not confidence. Cockiness is never as trustworthy as real confidence. Confidence is quieter, it is deeper, it is more reliable. Cockiness is ignoring the circumstances; confidence is assessing the circumstances. Cockiness is a cover for our insecurities and fears; confidence is the strength to admit our fears and insecurities without succumbing to them. Cockiness is pretending that we are certain; confidence is admitting our uncertainty without diminishing our commitment. Cockiness is holding fast to the decisions that we've made (no matter how deep the water is!); confidence is re-evaluating our decisions when necessary and making the appropriate course corrections.

For Your Journal:

- *Have you ever had a friend or co-worker act cocky? What insecurities was s/he hiding? How did the cockiness affect you?*

- *Have you ever acted cocky because you were not confident? What insecurities were you covering? What happened?*

- *When do you feel most confident?*

- *What allows you to feel confident?*

- *How can you use your knowledge about your own past successes to fuel your confidence in the future?*

> *"Be ready at any moment*
> *to give up what you are*
> *for what you might become."*
>
> W.E.B. Du Bois,
> *American scholar, civil rights leader*

Section Two: Making Choices

Notes from My Journal

Self-awareness is a wonderful first step. But, it's not enough. So often I've known that I was making a poor choice, and yet still proceeded in the counter-productive or destructive action. What good does that do me? Or those around me? I mean, if I am aware of the fact that I am making bad choices but I do nothing differently, I am almost worse off than before! **I was no longer ignorant of my actions, so I couldn't continue to be oblivious of my choices.** This next step would require much more discipline.

Probably the hardest area for me was my temper. By the time I was eleven years old, I'd learned to be brutal with my anger. In an example of empathy gone horribly awry, I always had a great deal of insight into others' feelings, so when I was mad, I knew exactly how to say things that were cruel and hurtful. I seldom – if ever – missed my mark. While I am quite ashamed of that now, it was the only thing I knew. I learned it by watching some of the adults around me when I was a child. I thought that was how I was supposed to act, how I was supposed to stand up for myself.

However, as my awareness grew, I started recognizing how I was affecting people. I realized that that was simply not the person I wanted to be.

In order for me to choose differently, I had to develop discipline and self-control to walk away when I was mad. The first few times were brutally difficult! But, I began to notice that I could do it - and I was getting better results. I was no longer alienating everyone.

Making Choices | 33

The next step was to learn to be assertive, not aggressive (this did take practice!). I no longer felt so bad about myself. I began to like who I was and who I was becoming.

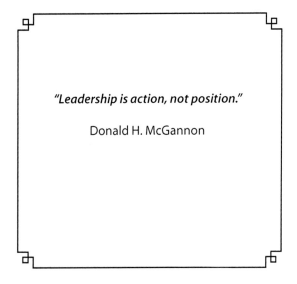

"Leadership is action, not position."

Donald H. McGannon

Values in Action

*"Values are like fingerprints. Nobody's are the same,
but you leave 'em all over everything you do."*

Elvis Presley

A couple of years ago, I was speaking at a national convention. After the program, one young man approached me and said, "You know, listening to you speak, I just get this feeling that anything is possible for me. I've been wanting to pursue a promotion at work, but I didn't know if I could do the job. Now, I'm going to do it. Thanks for believing in me." And with that he walked away. I was thrilled that he had gotten that from my presentation, but I was also puzzled. Nowhere in my presentation did I say, "Anything is possible for you" or "I believe in you." It is what I believe and it's what I want others to feel, but I hadn't said it.

Later that day, when I ran into the young man at lunch, I asked him how he knew those things when I hadn't said anything. He said, "You don't have to say anything. You just are." That is still one of the best compliments that I've received.

The compliment we want to hear the most is a reflection of what we value most. True happiness and fulfillment come when we have aligned our actions with our values. When we are not being true to who we are inside, we are out of integrity. But when we create the alignment, we gain incredible energy and clarity that flows naturally in everything we do. So when we get that great compliment – when people see our values alive in our actions – our values are rippling out in the world.

For Your Journal:

- *What are the greatest compliments someone could give you?*
- *Why are these important to you? What are the underlying values?*
- *Which is the most important to you? Why?*
- *How could you let that flow even more strongly into your daily actions?*

Communication is a Mirror

"Speech is the mirror of the soul; as a man speaks, so is he."

Publilius Syrus (Roman author, 1st century B.C.)

One of my high school teachers made a big impression on me. When she perceived that someone had stepped on her toes, she didn't ask them to get off. She got so mad that she verbally tore their legs off. I'm embarrassed to admit that I emulated her for many years. I thought that is how you stand up for yourself.

Eventually I learned that there is a difference between standing up for yourself and tearing the other person down. Standing up for yourself is about communication. Tearing someone down is about combat.

Standing up for yourself is about being true to yourself, including being sure that your communication reflects how you value those with whom you are interacting. The funny thing about communication is that it reveals far more about us than simply what we say.

The way we communicate is a reflection of our values, our beliefs, and our true feelings, as well as our skills. If the way we communicate is a mirror of our selves, I didn't like the person in that reflection, which is why I have relentlessly studied it for more than twenty years now. I found that my communication was getting in the way of being the person I wanted to be.

For Your Journal:

- ✧ What does your style of communication tell others about you? In answering, think about how you communicate with the important people in your life (spouse, children, friends, siblings, coworkers, boss, team – you may have different answers for each).

- ✧ How satisfied are you with those messages?

- ✧ For those areas where you are not satisfied, what gets in your way?

- ✧ Is there anyone with whom you would like to improve your communication?

- ✧ What could you change to get a better result?

Communicating from Values

*"By taking the authentic action,
you get the result that's right for you."*

Rick Fowler

I prefer communication that is very clean and clear; I don't like passive aggressiveness and I don't like blaming. A few years ago, I was faced with a very troubling situation: I began to feel uncomfortable with the way a good friend, Jan, was communicating with me. At first, it was just a passive-aggressive comment here or there. Because that wasn't Jan's normal routine, it surprised me and I let it go.

Like so many things that we try to ignore, the situation continued to get worse until it was truly a problem. One day, while my husband, Rick, and I were taking a drive, I brought the situation up, and I told him that I feared that if I addressed the situation, Jan would become defensive, and it would be the end of the friendship.

Rick raised the following two questions:

1) If Jan did react that way, was that really the kind of friendship I wanted?; and

2) Was I being true to myself and to Jan if I continued to ignore it?

Since I say I value clean, clear, authentic communication, it was time to put that value into action: to stand up for myself as cleanly and clearly as I could; no games, no judgments, no passive aggressiveness, and no insults. Jan might accept it or reject it; I didn't get to control the result, but I could control my actions and insure that they were in line with my beliefs.

For Your Journal:

- ✧   *Think about a situation where you needed to confront someone about an issue. How did you approach the situation; what did you do? How satisfied were you with the outcome?*

- ✧   *In reflecting on this situation, did your values guide your behavior? If so, how?*

- ✧   *If not, what do you think it would look like to see your values in action?*

Empowered Beings vs. Victims

"There is no tougher challenge that we face than to accept personal responsibility for not only what we are but also what we can be."

David McNally

I'm writing this on an airplane, returning from a speaking engagement. My topic was personal mastery. Part of my message was that we create our lives through the choices we make. After the presentation, someone suggested that some folks choose to be victims while some choose to be empowered. As I was boarding the flight, I was pondering that statement.

This plane has two seats on the left and three seats on the right; therefore, the overhead bins on the right are larger. The flight attendants were instructing us to put our roller bags in the bins on the right, which I did, and then I promptly took my seat, which was on the left side of the plane. I began to read. I heard the person across the aisle from the middle seat shouting, "Hey! Are you sitting on that side of the plane?" I thought it an overly hostile tone, but I politely replied that I was.

Raising his voice, he yelled, "Well, if you sit on that side of the plane, your bag goes on that side of the plane!!" I was unaware of this particular FAA regulation (and, apparently, so were the flight attendants). However, I could see this guy was really worked up so I politely pointed out what the flight attendants had said. Raising his voice yet another level (causing an ugly red flush on his face) he shouted,

"Oh, well, I guess you're just special! I guess I can just suffer and have my stuff on the floor!" Still polite, and somewhat confused as I didn't see any "stuff" at his feet, I replied that if there was something that he wanted to put in the overhead bin, I'd be happy to stow it for him. Shouting again, he said, "No! I'll just let my stuff get dirty. It'll be just fine!! I'll suffer!"

Apparently, he really wanted to suffer, and nothing I could say or do would change that. Sometimes people decide on a negative outcome and then make choices that insure that result. If we see ourselves as empowered beings, we make empowered choices. If we see ourselves as victims, we make choices that are self-sabotaging. We create what we believe.

For Your Journal:

- *Think of a time you made a choice from that victim perspective.*

- *How did that affect you and those around you?*

- *To what extent did you take ownership and responsibility of the situation and of the outcome? What or who did you blame or make responsible?*

- *What could you have taken responsibility for?*

- *Think about a time when you made an empowered choice. How did you feel about yourself? Did it help you to make similar empowered choices?*

Living Up

> *"Better to write for yourself and have no public, than to write for the public and have no self."*
>
> Cyril Connolly

As I've mentioned, in high school I took speech and debate. Our school had a long tradition of success in debate. The last great debater, Cindy, had graduated the year before I joined the team. Cindy had gone to the national competition several times and had done very well there. In our state, she was a legend.

Soon after joining the team, I was pegged as her successor, "the next Cindy." I had success on the team; I won trophies and tournaments, but I was no Cindy. Even though I was having success, I wasn't satisfied with it, and it felt like no one else was either. I wasn't living up to their expectations of me; I wasn't Cindy. Regrettably, when I graduated from high school, even with all the awards and tournaments I had won in speech and debate, I felt like I had failed. This is a trap that I have found myself in many times in my life: *I allowed other people's expectations of me dictate how I defined success for myself.*

Other people might be quite well-intentioned, but we cannot allow their expectations to define our goals. When we take on the expectations of others and make those expectations our goals, we give up control of our own life. We hand over the power of our own goals to someone else. At that point, we are not living our life; we are seeking to live a life that someone else prescribes for us. We can thank them for their caring and support, but we don't have to blindly take on their expectations.

We cannot let others' expectations of us become straitjackets.

For Your Journal:

- ✧ *What is your definition of success? To what extent does this grow from others' expectations?*
- ✧ *How do you remain true to that definition even in the face of judgment or criticism from others?*
- ✧ *How is your definition of success tied to your values?*
- ✧ *What's most important to you about your definition?*

Deal With What's There

*"How many legs does a dog have if you call the tail a leg?
Four. Calling a tail a leg doesn't make it a leg."*

Abraham Lincoln

When I enrolled in my undergraduate program, I was able to do a technology proficiency exam. If I passed, I would get credit for the course without actually taking the course.

When I first looked at the proficiency test, I was appalled. What a bunch of busywork! I don't mind work, but meaningless time wasters truly annoy me. At one point in my career, I handled all of the computer training for a 200+ employee law firm in Chicago. In that role, I wrote three computer manuals, provided training on Word-Perfect, Excel, and various other programs. I also did all of the Macro programming for the firm. With the technology proficiency exam, however, I would have to prove my expertise by showing I know how to bold a title.

I was whining about this (to myself) when it occurred to me that the folks at the university probably weren't going to change the rules of the game for me (no matter how stupid those rules were). It was what it was and the sooner I dealt with that reality the sooner I would get it done. In the end, I am ashamed to admit, I probably whined about it longer than it actually took me to do the exam (which I passed).

Making Choices | 45

There are many times in life when we are faced with something that we think is unfair or that "shouldn't be this way." We get stuck on the "it's unfair." We put all of our energy into why it's not fair when the fact of the matter is it doesn't matter if it's fair or not – it is what it is and we have to deal with it.

For Your Journal:

- *Have there been times when, faced with a situation that you thought was unfair (or ridiculous), you have been waylaid by those feelings? What happened?*

- *When you are faced with a situation that you believe isn't fair, how can you stay focused on solving the problem rather than debating the problem?*

Intention vs. Action

"You can't build a reputation on what you are going to do."

Henry Ford

As anyone who has ever started a business knows, the first few years are chaotic and busy. It is all-consuming. It was no different for me. I would put off answering emails from my friends and family because I was too busy. In truth, I felt guilty if I was doing anything other than working. I would buy birthday cards for my nieces and nephews and then be "too busy" to get them in the mail on time (or at all). After several years of this, my sister grew quite frustrated with me. She accused me of not caring about her or her kids. I was outraged! Of course I loved her and her kids – couldn't she see that? Didn't she trust me?

One day, I came across the following quote from the Disney Institute, which stopped me in my tracks:

"We judge ourselves by our intentions;

others judge us by our actions."

Ouch. Yes, my intentions were great, but then I looked at my actions, at those things that my sister could actually see. From that vantage point, I could see that she had a good case. I knew in my heart how much I loved her and her kids, but I wasn't showing that, I wasn't acting on the intention. I had a decision to make. Was it a priority to be a good sister and aunt? If that was a value, then what actions would that entail?

How many times have we said, or heard, something like the following: "Of course I love you – I'm just busy with work right now…," or "Of course your friendship is important, but you know how work is…," or "Of course you are a valued customer, I've just been busy…" When I hear myself saying the words "of course" in a context like this, they signal a red flag to me. Maybe I feel that something is important, but am I acting like it's important?

What do your actions say to those who are important to you?

For Your Journal:

- ✧   *What do your actions tell others about who you are?*
- ✧   *To what degree are your priorities showing up in your actions?*
- ✧   *What would you change?*
- ✧   *How can you begin those changes?*
- ✧   *What are some red flags for you that you might be drifting from your priorities?*

Finding Another Way

"Every situation, properly perceived, becomes an opportunity."

Helen Schucman

One night, after class, I was preparing to leave school. My class is on the 14th floor. As I got to the elevators, I could see a mass of people waiting for the elevators. It appeared that there was only one working elevator and the other ones were out of service. It was also readily apparent that many of the people waiting there were quite upset. I could hear people complaining about how upsetting it was that they had to wait for the elevators. They were getting quite irate.

I quickly walked by this group and went around the corner to another bank of elevators where I had no wait and was quickly on my way home. What I don't understand is why a person would rather stay stuck and complain when they could so easily solve their problem by simply adapting?

It is a fact of life – and maybe not a fact that we like: There will be times when the option that we most desire simply becomes unavailable to us. At those times, we need to look for other options, other solutions. I had a professor who said it this way: Maybe a child can sit and pout when things don't go his way, but an adult finds another way. If something isn't working for you, take a different action. It's empowering to realize that we don't have to be victims of the circumstances that arise.

It doesn't make sense to get upset and remain stuck when we have other options. They may not be our first choice, but they can still get us where we want to go!

For Your Journal:

- *Think of a situation where your first option was taken away from you. What happened? What did you do?*

- *Was it easy or difficult to find a second option? If it was difficult, what made it so? What role do feelings have in this process?*

- *Think of a situation you are facing now where you are unlikely to be able to "take your usual elevator." Can you think of three other options to get where you want to go? Six? Ten?*

- *How does it feel to identify numerous choices?*

- *How can you find options when others only find complaints?*

Intention + Effort

"Thought is the sculptor who can create the person you want to be."

Henry David Thoreau

I saw a news program called the "New Explorers" chronicling the recovery of three people who had suffered brain or spinal cord injuries. One man had suffered a spinal cord injury just below his chest and he was left a paraplegic. He remained confident and determined that he would one day walk again.

When he was sent home from the rehabilitation center he was still in a wheelchair, but he was coping very well. And, he still had faith that he would walk again. Within a few months, however, he became discouraged and stopped doing his physical therapy. Unfortunately, a blood clot formed in one of his legs and moved to his lungs; he was in the hospital for a couple of weeks but he recovered. They interviewed him during his recovery and he said that he had learned something that was very important through this experience: **not only do you have to have faith, you've also got to work for it.**

It's an important and relevant lesson for us all. I have seen many entrepreneurs who had faith that they would succeed, but, for some reason, they never got around to doing the work that would bring them closer to success. Likewise, I have seen entrepreneurs who worked hard, but who worked with a sense of impending doom, not impending success.

For Your Journal:

- *What actions should you be taking to support the faith you have in your own success?*

- *What actions are you actually taking?*

- *What fuels the faith that you have behind your actions?*

- *When working on something new, do you work on it with a sense of eventual success or a sense of eventual failure? And, why do you suppose that is?*

Holding On vs. Learning

> *"I've always felt that a person's intelligence is directly reflected by the number of conflicting points of view he can entertain simultaneously on the same topic."*
>
> Abigail Adams

Sometimes, I really dislike group projects, and I suspect I'm not alone. Most people have a horror story of a project run amok. Mine came in a training and facilitation project. Our group ran into trouble almost immediately. We had two women who immediately starting butting heads. Loudly. Forcefully. Disrespectfully. What became very apparent to me was that each of them had a different perspective on "the right way" (ironically, neither woman had experience in conducting training). Each woman was making the assumption that because the other woman had a different perspective than she did, that meant the other perspective was wrong. Not different, wrong.

Different doesn't necessarily mean wrong. Different means different! While it might be tempting to dismiss an idea or suggestion that is different, it's hard to learn new things and new approaches if we are more committed to holding on to what we know than we are to learning.

Over the years, I've worked to cultivate the discipline that when someone proposes something that is different from how I would do it, I ask myself questions: What can I learn from this perspective? What can I add to it? When would this be helpful? How does it build on what I already know?

Lifelong learning requires lifelong testing of what we think we know.

For Your Journal:

- *When faced with new information which conflicts with your current way of doing things, how do you react? Do you listen or do you automatically reject it?*

- *How can you challenge yourself to be curious about the new information: Do you fully understand it? What new "kernel of truth" might you find?*

- *Which of the following ideas would help you explore options:*

  - *Look for the overlap between the ideas: are there things common to both?*

  - *Look for what might be useful and helpful.*

  - *Seek a learning opportunity.*

  - *When you do reject new information, why? Is all the new information really irrelevant?*

  - *Sometimes, we resist accepting new information because of a fear. What is at risk for you in considering a different perspective? To what extent is that risk real versus fear?*

How Would Success Feel?

"The future is purchased by the present."

Dr. Samuel Johnson

When I was a junior in high school, I was asked to be a contestant in the Miss Teen Missouri pageant (it was based on my academic record). I laughed and thought, "no way." My mom took a look at the invitation and pointed out that part of the pageant was a speech competition. As I've said earlier, I had severe speech problems as a kid. As a result of those speech problems, I took a lot of teasing and abuse from the other kids in my class.

When my mother pointed out the speech portion of the competition, she said, "You know, I think it would be pretty amazing if, given the speech problems you had in the past, you were able to win this portion of the competition. I would think that if you were to win that portion of the competition, that might make the local newspapers. I wonder, how would that feel?" Well, I had to admit that that would probably feel pretty good. So, I entered the pageant and won the speech competition, and, yes, it did feel good.

Over the years, I have found myself using this mechanism to motivate myself. I think of the potential reward and then ask myself, "How would that feel?" For example, this past week, I had a number of complex projects to complete. I was not that excited about starting. I thought to myself that if I worked hard I could probably complete two of the projects by the end of the day. Then I thought to myself, "How would that feel?" I thought it would feel pretty good and was then motivated to work on them.

The key is to identify the positive reward, the positive pay-off of our efforts and to allow ourselves to anticipate the emotional reward.

For Your Journal:

- *Think of a time when you faced a project or task (or consider a present one). Brainstorm what your personal pay-off or reward might be (there could be more than one).*

- *Why are those pay-offs important to you?*

- *How does that (or could it) serve to motivate you?*

Meet Your Own Needs

"The strongest principle of growth lies in human choice."

George Eliot

Many years ago, I worked in a doctor's office. For the most part, I enjoyed the experience. However, over time, I became frustrated. I didn't like the way some of the communication was handled. I also thought that, in general, the office lacked leadership. We had one doctor, Dr. S., who was truly amazing and appreciative of all of our efforts. Unfortunately, we had another doctor, Dr. E., who, at best, was disrespectful of other doctors, the nurses and the entire staff.

One day I was visiting my parents and I was talking to my dad about the situation at the office. I was telling him how frustrated we all were with Dr. E., and that we were also frustrated with Dr. S. for not standing up to Dr. E. Eventually, when I stopped complaining, my dad said, "You know, you have been complaining about the same thing for months now. You are waiting for others to change to meet your needs. When are you going to take responsibility for your own needs and do something differently?"

I'm not sure how appreciative I was, at the time, for this bit of wisdom. However, within a few weeks, I had found a better job and was moving on. I have never forgotten this bit of wisdom from my dad.

Too often we are waiting for others to change or to rescue us.

The world will not change to meet our needs. We have to change to meet our needs. ***Our needs are our responsibility.***

For Your Journal:

- *Think of a situation which has consistently bothered you for several months. Describe the situation.*
- *What are three or more choices you have in this situation?*
- *Are you looking for ways to affect the change you need or are you waiting for the circumstances to change?*
- *If you are waiting, what leads you to wait?*
- *Is this a pattern for you? If so, how has this pattern affected you?*
- *What would make you feel more confident and comfortable in acting on your own behalf?*

Feeling vs. Acting

"What it lies in our power to do, it lies in our power not to do."

Aristotle

I once worked with a woman who would fly into rages on a weekly basis. Anyone in her path was vulnerable to her attacks. Once her anger was spent, she would expect everyone to forget her tirades. Her justification for her behavior was that she had experienced some emotion – anger, frustration, annoyance – and, therefore, there was nothing she could do about her actions. Was she right? If we feel an emotion is there truly nothing we can do about it?

Current neuroscience suggests otherwise: *Our thoughts and our feelings are what they are, our actions are what they are.* If we are faced with a rude sales clerk, we may feel annoyed or frustrated, and that is automatic (though partly a learned response). However, we have control over what happens next. We choose our actions, and we choose what feelings we escalate. We don't **have** to choose to retaliate by being rude back to the clerk. Of course, if our usual response is to hit back, it takes effort and practice to change.

Just because we experience an emotion doesn't mean we have to act on it. What a powerful concept: We can experience an emotion without becoming a prisoner of that emotion. I've found this reassuring. It gives me permission to experience a feeling or an emotion (for example, annoyance when someone cuts me off in traffic), but still retain personal power in choosing how I respond (for example, choosing not to throw a rock at the person who cuts me off in traffic… although, I admit that sometimes the thought of throwing a rock does cheer me up!).

As I've said, putting this in action has been challenging. But there are two keys that have helped:

There is a difference between emotion and behavior.

There is a space between feeling and acting.

I have implemented these keys by asking myself this question: Is the way I am about to act congruent with my values and the person that I believe myself to be?

For Your Journal

- *Think about a recent event where you experienced an intense emotion (anger, frustration, annoyance, etc.) involving either a co-worker, teammate, family member or friend. What happened to cause the emotion? How did you respond?*

- *After you had time to cool down and reflect on your behavior, how did you feel about your actions?*

- *How did this interaction affect your relationship with the other person involved?*

- *After the triggering event occurred, what could you have done differently which would have caused the interaction to go better?*

Doing the Work

*"Leaders aren't born they are made.
And they are made just like anything else, through hard work.
And that's the price we'll have to pay to achieve that goal,
or any goal."*

Vince Lombardi

Recently an acquaintance of mine, Brenda, commented about how much energy I seem to have. She told me that she was envious of my good health and my energy level. Brenda went on to tell me that she was listening to a CD by the latest guru on positive thinking. Accordingly, she was thinking positively and visualizing the result that she wanted. I told her that was a great start and I asked her, "And, what are you doing to get those results?" She looked somewhat confused and said, "Visualizing."

Therein lies the problem. I am a great believer in positive thinking and in visualizing what we want. I am also a great believer in doing those things that contribute to a positive result. Thinking isn't enough: Action is required.

In 2003, I collapsed and was extremely sick for months and I was in recovery for approximately four years. It was a long, slow, painful journey back to good health. When I was in the early stages of recovery, I visualized being healthy and strong again. I visualized being able to run and play tennis again. That was important, and insufficient. I also had to take action. That was critical. I had to make myself get up and go for short walks (at first, all I could do was make it to end of our driveway, but slowly that distance grew). I also had to take the 18 or so vitamins and supplements prescribed by my doctor. I educated myself on the illness and the recovery. I found a great team of healthcare professionals to help me. Today, I am in that very small percentage of people who experience a full recovery not just because I thought positively and visualized the recovery, but because I also did the hard work that the recovery required.

Positive thinking is good. **Positive thinking plus positive action is effective.**

For Your Journal:

- *Think about one of your goals. What does it look like to you? Write a detailed paragraph describing it.*
- *Why is it important to you? What would it mean if you had it or achieved it?*
- *List 10 actions that could lead you to the positive result you desire.*
- *Which is the first action to try?*

Discipline

"Opportunity is missed by most people because it is dressed in overalls and looks like work."

Thomas Edison

Discipline gets a bad rap. I've been accused of being disciplined a few times in my life and, each time, the accusation is made with disdain and scorn. However, I would argue that discipline is what makes me successful at the things I do.

Discipline is not a bad word. I don't even think about being disciplined; I just think about the result I want and the actions I need to take in order to get that result… and then I do those things. **Discipline is consistently doing those things which contribute to the desired result.**

For example, I have noticed that I feel at my best when I do yoga twice a week and go to the gym twice a week. I do best at school when I set aside time and do the reading and the homework. I remember when I took neuroscience, I was one of a handful of people who made an "A" in the class. After class one night, a bunch of us were talking and it turns out that the only people who made "A's" were also the only people who actually did the required reading. I don't think it's a big leap to think that there might be a connection here.

Many people think that discipline is about sacrifice. I disagree: Discipline is about gaining that which we most desire.

For Your Journal:

- *What is it that you desire most?*
- *What are the behaviors and actions that you need to take in order to get the result that you want?*
- *What are you doing – every day – that will move you closer to the results you desire?*
- *If you think of discipline as meaning sacrifice, how can you re-frame it as merely being a tool to use to gain what you desire most?*

Indulging in Tantrums

"People who fly into a rage always make a bad landing."

Will Rogers

I once had a friend who would always lose her temper as though she had no control over it whatsoever. To hear her talk, you'd think that someone came in and took over her body and mind and caused her to act like a madwoman. She never took any responsibility for these tirades. To make matters worse, once she calmed down, she would put it on the other person to forgive her. She would say something like, "I can't help it if I lost my temper, and you will just have to deal with it." Wrong on both counts.

While sometimes we all get mad, it's a choice to have a tantrum. Admittedly, sometimes it's a very difficult choice to remain calm, but it is always a choice.

When people act this way they are not thinking about the consequences beyond the immediate gratification of telling someone off. This is self-indulgent. As I've said, there was a time when I had a very nasty temper. I thought that I had to explode, and in those moments my own anger was the only thing that mattered - as though having a tantrum was some divine right that had been given to me. As soon as I made the connection that it was a choice, and therefore, something I had control over, I began to re-frame the way I looked at things. I trained myself to think beyond the immediate and instead consider all the ramifications of my actions.

Losing your temper is self-indulgent.

For Your Journal:

- ✧ *Think of a situation where you lost your temper.*

- ✧ *What were the intended consequences of your actions? (e.g.., "I would feel better by telling someone off.")*

- ✧ *What were the unintended consequences of your actions? (e.g.,., "I still have to work with this person," "I might seriously damage this relationship," or "This might affect other people besides just me.") Do you really want those results?*

- ✧ *If a similar situation arises, is there a way to talk about the problem that moves toward solution rather than demolition?*

Focus

> *"The people who hate you don't win*
> *unless you hate them – then you destroy yourself."*
>
> Richard Nixon

When I was in the 6th grade, I was on the volleyball team and the softball team. I was a cheerleader. I took guitar and piano lessons. I was in the choir. I took dance and gymnastics lessons. I even took diving lessons. I was reasonably good at all these things. I began to notice that every activity I joined, my nemesis, Sheri, joined (or, at least, tried to join). It was no secret that she intensely disliked me and I returned that favor.

After a while, it began to annoy me that she was trying to join everything that I was doing. I began to obsess about what she was doing. I began to get distracted from my own activities, and I felt like I wasn't performing to my full capability. Of course, I blamed this lagging performance on Sheri ("clearly" it was her fault).

One night over dessert, I was complaining to Mom about Sheri and I was trying to figure out what to do about her (I guess I was hoping for permission to demolish her). My mom's response was quite disappointing. She told me to simply forget about Sheri, to completely ignore her existence and focus only on my stuff and doing well at it. It wasn't exactly the evil strategy I was hoping for, but I decided to give it a try.

It taught me an invaluable lesson in life: you cannot control what someone else is doing (or trying to do) but you can control what you are doing. By simply focusing on my own activities, I left Sheri way behind.

There's a reason why horses in a race wear blinders – so they stay focused on the finish line and aren't distracted by what's going on around them. It's important that we stay focused on what's important and tune out the meaningless distractions.

For Your Journal:

- *Do you find yourself obsessing about what others are doing? If so, to what result?*

- *Instead of focusing on the external – what others are doing – what would it look like if you shifted your focus to what you are doing? What would that require of you? How would that improve your performance?*

Through the Fear

"Decide that you want it more than you are afraid of it."

Bill Cosby

As a kid, I was highly competitive, and I was lucky in that I did most things pretty well the first time I tried them. Speaking was the exception. Because of the speech problems I had as a kid, I hated speaking in front of people, I was deathly afraid of the ridicule that I knew would come from my awkward attempts.

But I was tempted. I silently watched some of the experienced speakers at my high school, and I would marvel at how articulate and graceful they were with their words. Secretly, I wanted to have that skill; secretly, I wanted to be like them; secretly, I wanted to try. I was terrified. I knew that speaking would be that thing that wouldn't come easily for me. I knew that I would probably fail quite a bit before I got it right. I knew that I had to risk being ridiculed and made fun of if I were to learn to do it and do it well.

I finally decided to try. My first year, I didn't even travel to tournaments. I practiced in front of my class and teacher, Mr. Jordan. Early on, Mr. Jordan told me that he thought I had more potential than any of the other students, but that I would have to work the hardest to bring that potential to life.

He worked with me on timing, making me stop and begin all over again when I began talking too fast (which was pretty much all the time). He would stop me – in the middle of my presentation – every time I said a word incorrectly (and then he'd help me get it right). Because my gestures were wild and nervous swoops (and a really hard habit to break), he would carefully tape my arms to a chair and that's how I would have to practice my presentation to the class. It was painful work. When I won my first tournament, I knew it was worth it.

How sad I would be if I had allowed that fear to stop me. We want to do things right. We want to do things well. That's admirable. However, what happens when we don't try something new or something that we are secretly passionate about because we are afraid? If that fear stops us, we leave our potential untapped.

For Your Journal:

- *What are some areas in your life where you allow fear to stop you from trying, or where you let fear limit you from fully committing?*

- *How would you feel if you took the risk? What are some benefits of moving past the fear?*

- *What's one risk you're ready to take now?*

Acceptance vs. Resignation

*"Acceptance is not submission;
it is acknowledgement of the facts of a situation.
Then deciding what you're going to do about it."*

Kathleen Casey Theisen

When I was twenty-five, I developed asthma. The specialist who confirmed the diagnosis painted a rather bleak picture of what I could expect from the disease. He gave me a book to read that outlined – in some great detail – the limitations I could expect. I wasn't pleased with what I read, so I consulted a second specialist who said essentially the same thing. Not satisfied, I consulted a third specialist.

He said something different. He told me that yes, I had asthma and asthma involved certain pitfalls and potential limitations. He said my asthma was serious and I had to take precautions and be careful. However, as long as I was willing to accept that and take the necessary precautions, there were things that I could do that could possibly improve my condition.

That was all I needed to hear! We worked out my exercise plan, which included running. I had never been a runner but I thought if it could help me combat asthma, I would give it a try. I had to take two different inhalers before going to the track and I had to run with one inhaler in my hand in case I had an attack (which, at first, was common).

My first time out, I proudly ran a quarter of a mile before gasping to an end. Within a couple of months, I was up to a mile. I practiced until I could consistently run the mile without needing the emergency inhaler. Then we started adding distance and intervals to build my lung capacity.

My doctor was with me every step of the way, counseling me on when to add distance and when to cut back on my two pre-run inhalers. By the time I turned thirty-five, I no longer had asthma.

There's a monumental difference between accepting a problem and resigning ourselves to that problem. I accepted that I had asthma. But, I didn't resign myself to it. I didn't give up hope.

Hope is essential. Scientists are now studying hope and what they have found is that hope is an essential element leading to action. When we believe in a positive outcome for our future, we are more likely to take actions toward that positive outcome. (And, of course, without positive action, hope is merely wishful thinking.)

For Your Journal:

- ✧ *What is the distinction between "accepting a problem" and "resigning yourself to the problem?"*

- ✧ *What is one challenge or difficulty where you've resigned yourself? What would happen if you switched perspective to accepting it and committing to action?*

Perseverance

"It's not that I'm so smart, it's just that I stay with problems longer."

Albert Einstein

I was in a new building, and the women were complaining about the lack of hot water in the restroom. When I went to wash my hands, I had the faucet turned all the way to hot. Nothing but ice cold water. So I turned the faucet all the way to cold. Scalding hot water. Could it be that I am the only one who tried turning the faucet the other way? Every time I use that sink, the faucet is turned all the way to hot (which, of course, dispenses the ice cold water).

With this on my mind, I began to notice how people react when their first option doesn't work: they appear stymied and they give up. Maybe it's because my first option so rarely works, I always think that there is another option, another way to get the result I want.

I'm also an optimistic person, which helps me to persevere and look for other options or new ways of doing things. Being optimistic, doesn't mean that I ignore the water being cold or that I pretend I like to wash my hands in ice cold water! Being optimistic means that I have confidence in my ability to achieve the desired outcome and I take responsibility for creating that result, instead of waiting for someone else to solve it.

I am convinced that one key to success is to keep thinking and keep going after others have given up. I don't know of any successful people who sit and wait for others to tell them the answers; they take responsibility for finding the answers that are right for them.

For Your Journal:

- ✧ What's your version of twisting the faucet in the opposite direction?

- ✧ When faced with an obstacle, what is your initial response?

- ✧ Do you look for alternatives? When do you look for alternatives and when do you have a tendency to give up? (Think about a few examples of both.)

- ✧ If you look for alternatives, would you say that you are realistic, and eventually, successful in those alternatives? Are there times when you remain persistent in your pursuit long after it is beneficial? What happened and what did you learn from that?

- ✧ If you tend to not look for alternatives, what do you think stops you? What could you do differently in the future that would lead you to seek successful solutions?

Jealousy

> *"Where you see valid achievements or virtue being attacked, it's by someone viewing them as a mirror of their own inadequacy instead of an inspiring beacon for excellence."*
>
> Vanna Bonta

Last summer, Rick and I spent a couple of weekends renovating our backyard here in Chicago. This required tearing out some grass to form a new planting bed and to reshape and enlarge one border area. Rick was able to create some beautiful sweeping curves with these planting beds. Next, we visited our local nursery and had a blast picking out 100 or so plants. Then, of course, we planted and mulched.

The result is wonderful! We like to sit out in our backyard and grill and we love being surrounded by beauty. We now have a beautiful place to sit outside, enjoy the evening, talk and have a glass of wine.

One of our neighbors is very envious of our yard. Even before this latest project, we had a very nice yard that we keep well-maintained. While neither of us enjoys weeding, we enjoy not having weeds. We also mow a couple of times a week, as needed. What's interesting about our neighbor is that she wants the yard that we have, but she doesn't want to do the work that we do. I see this phenomenon all the time: people are envious of something that someone else has but they only see the achievement, not the work that went into it.

When I see someone else with a nice yard or a beautifully designed kitchen or a thriving business, I don't envy them their successes; instead, I think, "I wonder how they did it? What can I learn from them? Where did they get their knowledge?" I look at them as a source of learning, not of envy. If I do ever feel envy, I ask myself: am I feeling envious because I have some unexpressed goal that I am not acting on, but could be?

For Your Journal

- *Think of a time when you experienced a twang of envy. Was it related to an achievement that someone else earned? Look at the emotion you felt: what is it really trying to tell you? (Is there some unexpressed goal that you have that the other person has achieved?)*

- *Is there something – realistically – that you could do that would move you towards your goal?*

- *If you feel envy of another, how can you redirect that to be a source of learning?*

- *Look around you. Find one person who you see as successful. This can be in the business you want to be in or someone who enjoys great relationships with others or someone who communicates well. Take a good look at that person and ask yourself: What are they doing that I could be doing?*

- *If I truly want the prize, how can I build the behaviors and habits that I need?*

Commitment

> *"Unless commitment is made, there are only promises and hopes; but no plans."*
>
> Peter F. Drucker

Desire: *to wish for, to long for, to want*

Commitment: *the trait of sincere and steadfast fixity of purpose; the state of being bound to a course of action*
(wordnet.princeton.edu)

Many times our desire fuels our commitments, but desire without commitment will likely end in disappointment. Think about how many times you hear people express their desires: "I want to lose weight," "I would love to own my own home," "I wish that I could make more sales," "I wish I were in better shape." These are all desires. They are wishes. Nothing wrong with having desires and wishes. But, what actions do you put around those desires?

    One of my commitments is good health. To me that means that I eat right (I splurge now and then), I drink approximately 100 ounces of water per day, I go for one long run once a week, I do interval training twice a week (at least), I bike or walk instead of drive when possible, I do yoga every other day (and I incorporate strength training with my yoga). I've taken my desire for good health and made commitments to myself.

Think about it for a minute: how many people do you encounter who want the prize (whatever that might be) but they don't want to put in the work and commitment to earn that prize? If the prize isn't earned, what is it worth? If we don't have to put a little bit of ourselves into it, how valuable can it be?

What are the actions that will lead you to your goals and desires? If you want to make more sales, for example, what are the actions that you need to take? Once you identify those actions, put them on your schedule. Actions – persistently taken – lead to results.

For Your Journal

- *Do you have desires or commitments?*
- *What deserves to be a commitment and not a mere wish?*
- *What is your path - the actions and behaviors – to fulfilling those commitments?*

Anger vs. Temper

*"Do not teach your children never to be angry;
teach them how to be angry."*

Lyman Abbott

When I was thirteen, our neighbors, Mae and Bea, went on a two-week vacation to visit family in California. They asked us to watch their farm for them. They had 8 sows (all of whom had the audacity to have litters in these two weeks), 30 or so chickens, about 20 head of cattle, and dogs and cats. One day during this time, my mom and little sister and I were out in our garden picking beans, when a pick-up truck roared into our driveway. Mr. Miller – whom I had never met – jumped out of his truck and came running toward us yelling and screaming. From what I could gather, Bea's bull had knocked over a portion of the fence separating their two pastures and, well, had become friendly with one of Mr. Miller's cows.

With the commotion, our dog, Snuggles (who was 75 pounds and not as friendly to strangers as the name would imply) came running out to meet Mr. Miller. Snuggles stood at my mom's side snarling and growling with his teeth bared. Mr. Miller demanded, "Will this dog bite?" My mom replied, "I really don't know but it looks like we might find out." With that, Mr. Miller ran back to his truck. When my dad got home from work, we told him all about it and he could see how upset we were.

We then heard a car approaching and Mr. Miller once again tore into our driveway. Once again, he hopped out of his truck yelling and screaming. This time, however, he wasn't greeted by Snuggles. He was greeted by my dad (who had been a boxer while in the Navy). By the look on Mr. Miller's face, he would have preferred Snuggles. He started running back to his truck yelling, "I ain't got no beef with you! I ain't got no beef with you!"

My dad – without appearing to run or even move fast – caught him at the door of his truck and said with chilling dead calm, "Well, I've got a beef with you. You need to understand one thing: Don't ever show up at this farm again raising your voice to my wife and kids. Never. Is that understood?" At this point, Mr. Miller managed a sweaty nod (I thought he was going to cry). My dad then calmly said, "Good. Now, let's talk about this problem with the bull and how we can fix it."

I was stunned! It was clear that my dad was very angry (he never really got angry so this was unusual). It was also clear that he didn't lose his temper. At the time this happened, I had a terrible temper. I remember watching my dad and thinking that maybe I could learn to deal with my anger without losing my temper. It was the first time that I had any awareness that it was even possible (unfortunately, that awareness didn't lead to overnight transformation!).

To be clear: It is okay and even healthy to feel anger. It is a perfectly normal emotion. It's okay to express anger. The art is in learning *how* to express it appropriately and not just explode like a bomb. Anger should be a signal to us that there is something that we need to address.[†]

For Your Journal:

- *Many people don't like to feel anger, and therefore, they merely suppress their anger without paying attention to what their anger could be telling them. Looking at times when you have recently felt anger, what did you do? Did you try and "make it go away" or did you seek to understand why you were angry?*

- *Do you rule your anger or does your anger rule you?*

- *If you feel like your anger is ruling you, do you notice any patterns?*

*For example, when I allowed my anger to rule me, I began to notice that I was damaging the relationships that I had with my friends and co-workers. I noticed that people stopped being around me. I noticed that people stopped giving me feedback. I also noticed – much to my chagrin – that while I might, by sheer force of will and volume, win the battle, the battle kept occurring over and over and over again. That's when it occurred to me that I wasn't, in fact, winning the battle; **I was merely insuring that I was going to be repeating the battle.** These all indicated to me that I needed to change. What do you notice?*

† To learn more about anger, read *The Dance of Anger* by Harriet Lerner, Ph.D.

Action

Anger is a valid emotion. It is a signal to us that something is wrong. Next time you feel anger, take a break. **Tell yourself that it is okay that you feel angry.** And then listen to what your anger is trying to tell you. What is the real issue? What is really making you angry? Don't accept the superficial answer – probe for the real issue.

"Where We Are" vs. "Where We Can Be"

"Lincoln was not born with his face on Mount Rushmore."

– from the back jacket of *Lincoln's Virtues* by William Lee Miller

A year ago, I started playing Frisbee golf. Rick and I play on a 19-hole course. I believe my first score was something truly horrendous like 18 over par. Although I have thrown a lot of Frisbees in my life, the golf Frisbees are quite different and I had very little control over where they went. I had expected to be good at this sport, so I was a bit disappointed.

I kept playing even though I was clearly struggling. I kept paying attention to what the discs would do in certain conditions and I kept working on improving my throwing skills. I struggled to learn different ways of throwing and to see what worked in different situation. I have steadily improved and my best score to date is a 5 UNDER par! A year ago, I didn't have that knowledge and I could really only get that knowledge by suffering through the learning!

There's a big difference between where we are and where we can be. How many times have you tried something new and thought "I stink!" and vow never to do that activity again? It happens not just in our recreational activities, but it happens in our professional lives as well. For example, we try our hand at sales and we are – initially – lost! Of course we are. We haven't done it enough to be able to recognize the patterns. We don't know what to do when we face an objection

Making Choices | 83

(an obstruction). We don't know how to avoid those objections in the first place. However, if we keep playing – and paying attention – our experience pays off and we learn. Before long, we are confident and competent.

The statement about Abraham Lincoln has long been one of my favorites. It's a powerful reminder that even a great man and recognized leader like Lincoln wasn't born that way. He had to work at becoming great. What a tragedy it would have been if he had taken one of his many failures as final and given up. I've studied Lincoln quite a bit and what is remarkable about him is that while failure may have temporarily disappointed him, it never stopped him. He zealously learned from every failure and every setback. What a tragedy it would be if any of us were to mistake any of our failures as final and give up.

For Your Journal

- *What greatness awaits you if you choose to persist?*

- *How can you disengage yourself from failure so that you can accept the lesson that's waiting? In other words, how can you use your own experiences to become a zealous learner?*

Emotional Assumptions

*"Begin challenging your own assumptions.
Your assumptions are your windows on the world.
Scrub them off every once in awhile, or the light won't come in."*

Alan Alda

I was recently at a seminar on leadership and emotional intelligence. Someone in the group, Bob, shared a story of how years ago he worked with a boss who he greatly admired. One day Bob presented the results of a project to his boss. The results were positive and even better than they had expected. However, Bob could tell that his boss was troubled. Bob assumed it was about the project and the results. Bob left the meeting feeling somewhat apprehensive. He stewed over it the whole day.

Finally, at the end of the day, he went back to his boss and said "Look, I can tell that you are upset over the results, and I think we need to talk about it." His boss looked at him and said, "What are you talking about?" Bob said, "I could tell that you were troubled when I gave you the results earlier." His boss replied, "Yes, I was troubled. But, not about the results. My son was in an accident yesterday, and while he is okay, I know that he was acting recklessly and I just don't know how to get through to him."

People have an innate ability to sense the emotions of others. What we have trouble with is accurately interpreting what those

emotions mean.

We often sense an emotion and we assume that it is directed at us. The good news in Bob's story is that at least he went back and talked to his boss about it in a calm manner. What he learned from the experience is that he had to check his assumptions. It would have been very easy for Bob, when he sensed his boss was troubled, to say something like, "It seems like you are troubled. Is it about the results or something else?"

For Your Journal:

- *Think about a time when you witnessed someone's behavior and then made assumptions as to motivation and intent. What happened?*

- *How do you – or can you – recognize when you are making assumptions about people, situations or behaviors?*

- *What can you do to test those assumptions before acting on them?*

Changing Our Patterns

> *"The greatest revolution of our generation is*
> *the discovery that human beings,*
> *by changing the inner attitudes of their minds,*
> *can change the outer aspects of their lives."*
>
> William James

The other day, I was talking with a group of people about our behavioral patterns and how some events trigger certain responses in us. I asked the others to name one trigger and how they typically reacted.

One man shared that he was the youngest of several children. As such, in his family, he was always treated like the baby – even now when he is nearly forty years old. He believes this is why others in the family always dismiss his ideas. When he senses that he is being treated this way, he reacts with frustration and anger. He tries to assert himself. As we talked, he admitted that this is a pattern that exists for him in his career as well. In his professional life, if his ideas are not readily accepted and implemented, he feels like he is being dismissed. Even though he is aware of this pattern, he said that he "can't help himself" from reacting with frustration and aggression even though this only causes more problems for him and his team.

He's making a critical mistake: he **can** help himself. He can choose a different response – and one that would be more beneficial to him and those around him. It's surprising to me how many people

Making Choices | 87

are aware of a pattern they have (which is a great first step) but they act as though they are a victim of it. They are not. Patterns can be changed.

We always hear that knowledge is power. It's not. Knowledge is only dormant power. ***It's how we act on our knowledge that determines whether it's power or folly.***

For Your Journal:

- *Identify one pattern (a trigger and your typical response) that you have that isn't producing a positive result for you, and write it down in detail. What happens, what is your typical response, and what is the result you get?*

- *What is the result that you actually want?*

- *What needs to change in your response in order to get that new result?*

> *"Nothing so conclusively proves a man's ability to lead others as what he does from day to day to lead himself."*
>
> Thomas J. Watson,
> founder of IBM (1874-1956)

Section Three:
Tapping Into Our Power

Notes from My Journal

Over the years, I learned a lot about myself. I learned about my behaviors and actions and how those things affected others and my relationships with them. I learned how to communicate. I learned to manage my emotions in a positive way. For me, however, something was missing. I remember a day back in the summer of 2000 when I thought "I have never been so not unhappy." That isn't a typo! What I meant is that for much of my life, I had been unhappy. Now I wasn't actively unhappy. However, on its own, that didn't make me happy. So, what was missing?

That began my next stage of the journey to discover meaning. What do I find fulfilling? What inspires me? What am I passionate about? What is my purpose?

These seem like overwhelming questions. That's why I came up with Core Operating Principles – they guide me in my daily behaviors and actions and when I'm choosing those things I want to become involved in.

Like the other phases of the journey, I imagine this is a lifelong quest. Finding meaning is a continually evolving process. What we care about and are passionate about today, will lead us to new opportunities and passions tomorrow. Something that was extremely helpful to me, and that I hope will be helpful to you, is a conversation that I had with one of my favorite professors, Donna. We were talking about what graduate school and which program I should attend. I had narrowed it down to a few choices. One stood out for me: Case

Western Reserve's Masters in Positive Organizational Development and Change. Donna listened to my selections and she agreed that Case was the best option for me. I worried out loud to her that I didn't know exactly what I would do with that degree. She said, "Bobbi, that program will prepare you for opportunities that you aren't even aware of yet. You can't even see what those might be yet. And, that's okay. The important thing is that you are following your passion, your interest and your energy. The application will come later." Wise words from a very wise woman. I hope that they inspire you as much as they have inspired me.

I Wish I'd...

> *"Twenty years from now you will be more disappointed by the things you didn't do than by the ones you did do."*
>
> Mark Twain

In 2005, I heard someone say that one way to set your goals is to think about those things that you would regret at the end of your life. For me, instantly what flashed into my mind, is that I would regret not finishing up my college career. I was the first in my immediate family to go to college; it simply wasn't something that was done. I finished my Associates degree with flying colors and was planning on pursuing my Bachelor's when a very dear friend was diagnosed with terminal cancer. I wanted to be there for him and his family. I thought it would be easy to pick back up at school; but then life happened! Years later, returning to school and getting my Bachelor's wasn't in the front of my mind, but, at hearing that question, it was what I thought of first.

Within a year of that experience, I was enrolled at DePaul University with a focus in Human Performance Improvement. I've continued with my studies, and will complete my graduate program in a few months. As this part of my travels comes to a close, it seems like it all happened in a heartbeat! It was fun and exciting; I've expanded my horizons and found contentment: I eliminated a potential regret.

For Your Journal

Imagine that you are approaching your 100th birthday. You look back over your life and reflect on the experiences that you have had:

- ✧ *What are you most proud of?*
- ✧ *Which experiences brought you the most happiness?*
- ✧ *Which experiences brought you the most satisfaction?*
- ✧ *Read what you have written above. What does that reveal about your values and priorities? What does it reveal about what's really important to you?*

*Again, imagine that you are approaching your 100th birthday. This time, you look back over your life and reflect on the experiences you **didn't have**. What did you leave out that you wish you could go back and include? In other words, what do you regret?*

- ✧ *What are those things that you have tucked away for "some day?"*
- ✧ *Is it time to take those out, dust them off, and pursue them today?*

Action

I have found it helpful to have a little list in the last page of my journal. This space is reserved for those times when I find myself wistfully thinking about things I could do or might have done. I record them and then I let them sit for a bit. What I find is that sometimes these are truly important to me and are in line with my values and priorities. In that case, I seek to integrate them into my life. I often find, however, that they are things that I don't long for or value so much as they are simply things that represent ideas and possibilities. In that case, I leave them on my list and revisit them later.

> *"Though no one can go back
> and make a brand new start,
> anyone can start from now
> and make a brand new ending."*
>
> Carl Bard,
> *Scottish theologian and broadcaster*

Gifts in Adversity

> *"If you will call your troubles experiences, and remember that every
> experience develops some latent force within you,
> you will grow vigorous and happy,
> however adverse your circumstances may seem to be."*
>
> John Heywood

Back in 1980, my family and I lived through a brutal drought. Not only was it forty dry days, but also the temperatures soared well over 100 degrees. We watched our crops wilt and die in the hot sun.

One day my dad and I were out surveying the damage in our garden, and we stumbled upon the watermelon plants that we had planted with anticipation of the sweet fruit they would bear. They should have been full sized by then, but the few melons left were not much bigger than cantaloupes. My dad reached down and pulled a couple off the vine and said, "I can't imagine that these will be any good now, but at least maybe our chickens will enjoy them." We walked over to the chicken pen and Dad tossed one of the melons into the pen. It split open as it hit the ground and Dad noticed that it was the most intensely red watermelon that he'd ever seen. So he decided to take the other watermelon inside. We eagerly watched as he cut it open. It was the sweetest, juiciest and most tender watermelon that we'd ever had. We called it our surprise gift from the drought.

Our lives are full unexpected gifts, even (or maybe especially) in times of challenge and struggle. Yet sometimes it's hard to see the gifts because they look different from what we expected. I wonder how many of our internal strengths go ignored?

For Your Journal:

- *When have you found an unexpected gift in a challenging situation?*
- *How did you come to recognize that gift?*
- *Do you have any gifts that you're ignoring or not appreciating?*
- *How could you use your gifts more fully?*

Giving Feedback

"To lead people, walk beside them."

Lao-tsu, Chinese philosopher

I was at a McDonald's recently and overheard a manager providing feedback to one of the employees. The feedback was a vague, "You did it wrong." At which point, the employee tried something different which garnered a new response, "Still not right!" This went on for several minutes with both parties becoming increasingly frustrated.

In contrast, I remember when I took diving lessons as a kid. I loved diving! I would spend the whole day practicing. My mom would come over to watch me and provide feedback. Her feedback sounded like this, "Your knees were slightly bent," or "Your toes weren't pointed," or "You didn't quite finish the rotation." And, there were many times when she said, "Ah, now you've got it!"

The way that she provided feedback taught me a lesson that has been valuable to me: if we're going to give helpful feedback, we need to make specific observations. Vague criticism doesn't help anyone get better.

For Your Journal

- ✦ *Think about a time when you received vague criticism from someone. How did it make you feel about the feedback and the person providing it?*

- ✦ *Did the fact that it was vague make it difficult to know what to do to improve?*

- ✦ *Look back on the last few times that you have given someone feedback. How did it go? Did they understand or were they still confused?*

- ✦ *What could you have done differently in those situations to help the other person understand how to improve?*

Listening to Understand

"Deep listening is miraculous for both listener and speaker. When someone receives us with open-hearted, non-judging, intensely interested listening, our spirits expand."

Sue Patton Thoele

I had just finished facilitating a group when someone came up to me and said that they admired my listening skills. They felt like everyone was heard and that I was able to help them cut through the clutter and get to the real issues. They asked me what I do to be a good listener. I thought about it and I came up with the following four factors (there may be more, but these jumped out at me):

1. When someone else is speaking, I am simply trying to understand the **real** question that is being asked. Often people are trying to ask a question, but they have difficulty articulating what they really want to know. If you can help them articulate the real question, the answer is a lot easier to find.

2. Likewise, people often have difficulty articulating what they really mean. If we are not truly seeking to understand what they mean, we end up having a conversation that never gets to the real issue. Often the real meaning is hidden underneath the words, so listening isn't just a matter of intellectual understanding, but something deeper.

3. I'm not afraid to say I don't have the answer. If we have an attachment to having an answer, it's tough to listen to the person talking. I'm not afraid of saying, "I don't know, let's explore it."

4. I'm not listening to influence; I'm listening to understand. There's a big difference. If we show up in the conversation with an attachment to the outcome, or with a private agenda, then it's tough to really listen. When I think I understand, I check with the other person to see if he or she feels understood.

For Your Journal:

- *How would you rate your listening skills?*
- *What sort of feedback do you get from others about your listening?*
- *What is your best listening skill?*
- *What one area could you improve that would make you a better listener?*

Contribution

*"Do you know what my favorite part of the game is?
The opportunity to play."*

Mike Singletary, Hall-of-Fame Football Player

On a farm there are some unpleasant jobs that just have to be done. We raised rabbits for both show and sale so we had a few hundred rabbits. The rabbit buildings needed cleaning on a weekly basis and, in short, the work consisted of raking, shoveling and hauling the manure out of the buildings. Someone had to do that job, and, when I was 14, that someone was me.

One hot summer day, I was pondering why I had been chosen for this job. It's hard to find meaning in a pile of manure, but it's what I had to work with. As I worked, I thought that if the manure wasn't removed, it would become a breeding ground for diseases. I knew that if one rabbit were to get sick, they would all be at risk.

Soon, I began to see my job not as a manure-shoveler but as someone who took care of the rabbits and made sure they stayed healthy. I was a Rabbit Health Care Practitioner. Now that was a role I could embrace. I knew that the rabbits provided us with a stream of income that was important to the family; I also happened to love the rabbits and didn't want anything to happen to them. I felt proud that I was contributing to something that was important to my family.

Recognizing that contribution made all the difference in my attitude. Every Saturday morning as I headed out the door for my job, I no longer said "I'm off to shovel the manure." Instead I said: "I'm off to take care of the rabbits."

Tapping Into Our Power

This change in attitude paid off the following year when we faced a severe heat wave. Local farmers were losing livestock to the heat (it was over 105 degrees for about 40 straight days). I was determined that I would not lose a single rabbit. After all, my job was to take care of them. In the heat of the afternoon sun, when they suffered the most, I would take buckets of ice out to the rabbit buildings and I would fill their ceramic drinking crocks with the ice. The rabbits would curl themselves around the crocks as a way to cool themselves. It worked. I didn't lose a rabbit! One day, my dad came home early and he caught me with my ice buckets. He asked me what I was doing and I told him. He looked at me, puzzled, and asked, "Who told you to do that?" I said, "No one, but I wanted to take care of the rabbits." My dad thought it was quite ingenious!

If I had viewed my job as merely a manure-shoveler, would I have made that extra effort? No way. That's the value of understanding the real contribution that we make: commitment to the outcome.

For Your Journal:

- *How does what you do positively affect others? (Think about all the areas in your life where you make contributions through your time and effort.)*

- *How can you re-frame an unpleasant task so that you look past the unpleasantness of the job and instead take pride in the contribution you are making?*

- *How can you help others find meaning and value in their everyday tasks?*

Is it Your Issue?

> *"No person is your friend who demands your silence,
> or denies your right to grow."*
>
> Alice Walker

It's amazing where you find wisdom in life.

My little nephew, Dylan, is ten years old. He's a bright kid, very sharp and personable. He has many friends. He has one friend who is also his neighbor. It appears that this friendship has some levels to it: when they are at either of their houses, they are great buddies; when they are at school, the other boy ignores Dylan; when they are on the school bus, the other little boy tries to make fun of Dylan. My sister, Kathy, asked Dylan how he was going to handle it.

Dylan replied that there was nothing to handle. He explained to his mom that he understood why his friend acted the way he did: his friend was a little insecure and nervous around the older, cool kids and that this was just his way of trying to fit in. Kathy asked Dylan if it didn't bother him to be made fun of. Dylan looked surprised and then said: "No. It's not my issue – it's his. He's the one that doesn't feel good about himself." It's powerful to recognize when something is your issue and when it's not.

Most of us encounter others who, at some level, try to suck us into their challenges and struggles. There are essentially two categories of this behavior. The first is the person who simply doesn't know how to solve their own problem. Many of us get drawn in, feeling like we're "helping" or "taking responsibility" when it just isn't ours to take. In situations like these, it's good to assess whether we are truly the best person to help. It's okay if we are not. We are NOT responsible for everyone's problems. The second category is people who are taking their problems out on us. In this case, it is important to recognize that solving the problem is not their intent: dragging you down into their abyss is the goal. In that case: stay clear of the trap. You can spend precious days of your life in someone else's pit of misery. **Choose** which issues – and which abysses – you step into.

For Your Journal

- ✧ *Think about a time when you experienced something similar to the story above. What were the circumstances? What happened?*

- ✧ *Were you able to maintain your perspective? Did you get drawn into the other person's issues? If you got drawn in, what was that experience like?*

- ✧ *What could you do differently in the future that would help you understand the other person without becoming enmeshed in their issues?*

Giving Instructions

*"The average teacher explains complexity;
the gifted teacher reveals simplicity. "*

Robert Brault

When I was about nine years old, my dad decided that it was time to paint our garage. Being a curious kid, I wanted to know why. He showed me where the paint had started to peel and he told me that painting would help protect the wood from the upcoming winter weather. I volunteered to help. I always loved helping my dad. I was definitely a Daddy's Girl and he was a very good teacher. He welcomed my help in painting the garage (or, at least, that's what he told me). He took me over to the wall that I was going to paint. He showed me how to stir the paint and he explained that I would need to stir it every so often. He then showed me how to hold the brush, how to dip it in the paint and get just the right amount, how to get rid of the excess paint, and finally how to actually paint the wall. He stood next to me as I started painting. Once he was confident that I had the hang of it, he went over and started painting.

Contrast that with a friend of mine who had a similar experience, except that my friend's dad simply said, "Paint the garage." My friend's dad didn't explain why, and certainly didn't talk through all the steps that go into painting – as a result, while I came to value the experience, my friend resented the whole thing and did a pretty poor job.

Once we understand how to do something, we group little steps together (prep the wall); however, someone who is just learning needs to have all those steps outlined for them (wash the wall, scrape the wall, spackle the wall where necessary, etc.). This is one of the most common mistakes that occurs when we are trying to train someone (whether formal or informal training). If we want someone to really get it then we have to help them understand all that goes into it - what, why and how.

For Your Journal

- *Have you ever found yourself frustrated that someone wasn't getting what you were telling them? Think about that experience. To what extent did you clearly convey the what, the how, and the why?*

- *Think about all the areas where you need to teach others what you know. Pick one of those and write down the instructions you would tell someone.*

- *Review your list of instructions. Read through it again and take a closer look at it: have you offered in one step something that's actually a cluster of activities? Would someone who has never done this activity before really know what you mean by it? For every cluster that you find, break down those steps.*

- *In the future, if others don't understand what you're teaching, how will you ensure that you're providing enough what, how, and why?*

Connecting

> *"Too often we underestimate the power of a touch, a smile, a kind word, a listening ear, an honest compliment, or the smallest act of caring, all of which have the potential to turn a life around."*
>
> Leo F. Buscaglia

A couple of years ago, we went to my aunt's house for Thanksgiving. There were about 20 of us there, only a few of my cousins and one of my sisters and her family. Jim, one cousin, was there; I had always thought that he wasn't a very talkative person. I was wrong.

Jim was going to college. He just got his Associate's Degree and he was working on his Bachelor's Degree. When Rick walked into the kitchen where Jim was watching over the turkey he was cooking, Rick said, "So, Jim, how's school going?" Jim's entire face lit up and he was off to the races!

By asking the question, Rick allowed Jim to talk about something that was important to him. I'm not sure the question was important to Rick; he asked it as generous person inviting someone to share. It's a gift that we all love to receive, but yet we aren't always good at giving it.

At dinner, Jim sort of asked me about my grades at school; he said, "I bet you make straight A's – you make me sick!" At that point, my sister said, "I don't even bother asking anymore, I already know the answer." It occurred to me that sometimes people ask us a question to learn the answer, and sometimes they ask to show they care. Maybe they already "knew" my answer, but if they'd asked, it would have acknowledged something important to me. So I committed to get better at asking questions, not just for information, but to deepen relationships.

The way that we ask questions – and listen to the answers – can help us build stronger relationships with our family, our teams, and our clients and our prospects.

For Your Journal

- *Do you ever find yourself **not** asking a question of others because you believe you already know the answer?*

- *Think about a time when there has been something important to you and yet no one else asked you about it. What was that like? How did you feel?*

- *By contrast, think about a time when someone has shown interest in something that was important to you? What was that like?*

- *How can you use questions as a way to show genuine interest in the other person?*

Getting More Data

"Assumptions are the termites of relationships."

Henry Winkler

Last week, I was taking the El downtown to meet a friend for lunch. I sat in a two-seater. However, when I looked down at the seat next to me, I noticed that there appeared to be gum on the seat so I didn't slide over to make room for someone else. Within a few minutes, I noticed a woman giving me hostile glances.

About ten minutes later, she approached me and angrily declared that I wasn't supposed to take up two seats. I pointed out that none of my stuff was in the seat and that she was welcome to sit there. She rather pointedly made a show of getting ready to assume her new seat. It was at that moment that she noticed the gum and said, "I can't sit in that seat – it has gum in it." At which point I said, "Yes. That's why I wasn't sitting in it." It was then that she became quite apologetic.

She wasn't a bad person. She just made a common mistake: she observed a behavior, made assumptions about the motive behind the behavior and then made a judgment. We all – at one time or another – make this mistake.

We could eliminate many misunderstandings if, instead of acting on our assumptions, we would take the time to test our assumptions and gather the real facts. When we test our assumptions and seek the real truth, we eliminate those regrettable moments when we act indulgently and end up looking foolish. Looking for the truth, and not just the surface assumptions, allows us to harvest the power that comes with self-management.

For Your Journal

- *Think about a time when you have observed someone's behavior and made assumptions about their motivation and intent. What happened?*

- *To what degree did you test your assumptions before acting? How could you have done better?*

- *Would you have gotten a better outcome if you had?*

- *How can you train yourself to distinguish assumptions from fact?*

Action: The next time you find yourself ascribing motivations to someone's actions, take a step back and ask yourself: Is this a proven fact or an assumption?

Acknowledging without Taking Responsibility

> *"The most precious gift we can offer others is our presence.*
> *When mindfulness embraces those we love,*
> *they will bloom like flowers."*

Thich Nhat Hanh

Last Summer I received a threatening e-mail from a stranger. It ominously alluded to the fact that he had been to my website and knew what I looked like and where I lived and that I would have no way of recognizing him should he approach me. It was scary. My rational side said that it was just a sick joke. My irrational side did the Charlie Brown yell.

As luck would have it, I received the e-mail the night before Rick was leaving town for the week on business. I had a class on Tuesday evening and I got home around 10:00. The best parking spot I could find was several houses away from mine. It seemed like a very long walk.

When I was safely locked inside my home, and, after checking the closets while carrying my trusted baseball bat, I phoned Rick. He was at a baseball game with clients. This didn't sit well with me: here I was facing certain death and he was at a baseball game! I told him – in somewhat colorful language – that I thought it was quite insensitive of him. There was a slight pause and then he said, "I understand that this is scary. I know that you are scared and you hate that. What can we do to make you feel safe?" Talk about diffusing a bomb!

This incident (and, yes, I know that I wasn't at my most reasonable) illustrates an important point about communication: it is almost always destructive to argue about a feeling (can you imagine where the conversation would have gone if Rick had told me that I was being silly for being scared?). Rather, you are much better off to acknowledge the feeling and then move the discussion to the real issue and to resolution.

To be clear, **you can acknowledge what someone else is feeling without taking responsibility for that feeling.** Look at how Rick handled it:

- He acknowledged that I was scared;
- He didn't tell me that I shouldn't have been scared; and,
- He moved us towards resolution ("What can we do to make you feel safe?").

The way he asked the question was key. Using the word "we" did two critical things: 1) it told me that I wasn't in it alone; and 2) it didn't shift the responsibility to Rick.

For Your Journal:

- *Think about a time when you have felt a strong feeling, such as fear, and someone came along and told you that you were silly for feeling that way and that there was no cause to be scared? What happened? How did you respond?*

- *How did you feel about the other person?*

- *Did their response help you deal with the feeling?*

- *What could the other person have done that would have helped you move forward?*

- *What can you take from this and apply in the future (i.e., when you're talking to someone with an "irrational" feeling, or when asking for help with one of yours)?*

Action

Instead of debating the validity of someone's feelings, acknowledge them. **You don't have to have the same feelings to do this, nor do you have to agree with their thinking and actions.** Acknowledge what they are feeling and then move the discussion forward. Dismissing what the other person is feeling will seldom – if ever – make their feelings go away. Instead, they are more likely to cling to their feelings all the more.

> "As human beings, our greatness lies not so much in being able to remake the world -- that is the myth of the atomic age -- as in being able to remake ourselves."
>
> Mahatma Gandhi

Moving Past Excuses

"It's not excusing what he did, but understanding what he did."

Robert Oswald (brother of Lee Harvey Oswald)

I was watching a program on the History Channel about the assassination of President Kennedy. They were interviewing Robert Oswald, who was talking about Lee Harvey and his various troubles. Robert made an important distinction: While we don't need to accept someone's behavior, and we don't need to excuse it, we are most powerful when we genuinely understand.

We can sometimes be very quick to hear one person's explanation of events as an excuse (and sometimes it is). When we do that, we cut off the conversation. However, if we listen carefully, can we gain a deeper understanding? Then can we use this insight to create a better outcome in the future?

I was working on a project with a virtual team, and our first week was rough. We were supposed to communicate via an online discussion board. We had made an agreement that we would all check in and contribute to the discussion at least twice per week. There were two people who did absolutely nothing. When we met the next week, these two started explaining to the rest of us why they had been unable to contribute. I was feeling impatient; I did the work, why couldn't they? I could hear myself thinking, "I don't want to hear your excuses," when Robert Oswald's quote came back to me.

Tapping Into Our Power

So I started to really listen to what they were saying. I asked questions, not to blame, but to discover. Once everything had been discussed, I asked, "So, how do we proceed as a team to make sure this doesn't happen again?"

While I still don't know if they were simply making excuses, we never had a recurrence of that problem.

I was pleased with the process and surprised by how well it worked. First, I didn't argue with their excuses. Second, I helped them express themselves, and by doing so I helped them to feel understood. *People simply will not budge in a conversation until they feel understood.* Third, I asked a future-oriented question that did two things: 1) it set the expectation that we wouldn't have the same problem occur in the future; and, 2) it moved the discussion to resolution.

For Your Journal:

- *Is there someone in your work or life who is making excuses about their performance?*

- *Instead of dismissing the excuses, how can you shift the conversation into deeper discovery?*

- *How can you ensure these people feel understood?*

- *What future-oriented question can you ask to set a clear expectation and move to resolution?*

Getting Deeper Connection

*"No one cares how much you know,
until they know how much you care."*

Don Swartz

One Sunday, Rick and I went to breakfast at one of our favorite diners here in Chicago. Brian, the kid who runs the register, had a cast on his right forearm and wrist. Rick said to him, "That looks painful. What did you do?" Brian responded, "Snapped a tendon." Rick tried again: "How did you do it?" "Playing basketball," was Brian's short response. Rick didn't give up: "Oh, that's really tough, isn't it? I remember getting injured playing a sport that I love." With that, Brian finally opened up and shared how it happened, when it happened, what it felt like, when he knew it was turning into a problem and that he had to have surgery to have it repaired.

This reminded me of something that I've heard many times: if you want to get to the real answer you need to ask at least three questions. We've gotten to a place in our society where we aren't really sure if the person asking the question actually cares about our response. Continuing to ask questions – and empathizing – shows that we do care. Caring opens the door to sharing, learning and growth. It also leads to trust.

There are two lessons for me in Rick's interaction:

First, it takes both perseverance and caring to form a deeper connection with someone. This is vital to positive relationships with those that we love. It's also important for relationships with our clients and our prospects and those on our team.

Second, if we're going to be people who connect with others in a positive way, we can do this everywhere. Brian isn't someone important in Rick's life or work, but Rick is choosing to see that Brian is important because he's a fellow traveler. This enriches both their lives.

For Your Journal:

- *When you ask questions, to what extent do you really care about the response?*

- *If you're staying on the surface and not truly connecting, why? Is it because you don't care, or because you're "being polite," or because you "don't have time," or are afraid, or something else?*

- *When you don't really listen to the answer, what do you think the other person might feel towards you?*

- *Think of a recent interaction that stayed on the surface. How could you have created a deeper connection by caring and asking? What value might have come from this?*

- *When someone demonstrates to you that they care about your ideas and opinions, how does that affect you?*

- *Would you like to add more of that in the world? How can you do so starting today?*

Time for Connection

"Action expresses priorities."

Mahatma Gandhi

Last summer I attended a certification program in Emotional Intelligence and Leadership at the University of Richmond's Business School in Virginia. It was a great experience and very enlightening about what makes an effective leader and what's at the heart of performance.

I was staying at the Embassy Suites and had the pleasure of interacting with one of the employees, Bobby. Bobby was the concierge and he also was the driver of the hotel's shuttle. I had made arrangements for the shuttle to take me to the University at 8:00 a.m. I arrived a few minutes early and sat in the lobby to wait. I noticed that as every guest came down, Bobby would greet them – by name! In addition to knowing all of their names, he knew something about what brought them to the hotel. "Oh, Mr. Lang, I hope you have a great presentation today!" It was magical to see how his words affected people: Each guest walked away from Bobby with a little more energy and a brighter smile.

Many of the guests told me they were often in Richmond on business and they never considered staying at any of the other hotels, even those that are far less expensive. Watching Bobby, I could see why. Bobby was simply and genuinely interested and caring for the

people who stayed in his hotel.

Most people want to strengthen their relationships – personally and professionally. Why is the "Bobby interaction" so hard? The usual answer I hear is "I don't have time," which is intriguing since it seemed to take Bobby just a few seconds.

So it's not truly a matter of time, it's a question of our priorities. **Every time we make a decision about how we spend our time, we are making a statement about what's really most important to us.**

For Your Journal:

- *Consider how you're spending time and how that reflects your values: Write down your priorities in one column. In another column, write down how you spend your time.*

- *What adjustments would you need to make so your time accurately reflects your priorities?*

- *How could you begin incorporating those changes?*

Lessons on Living

"And in the end, it's not the years in your life that count. It's the life in your years."

Abraham Lincoln

Last Fall, my cousin, Jimmy (age 46) was killed in a car accident. Apparently an oncoming car drove into his lane and he swerved to avoid it, lost control and was killed instantly as his truck rolled several times. It was unbearably sad. Jimmy was a veteran and had served his country for many years; he wanted to become a teacher. In pursuit of that goal, he was back in school and was working as a student teacher. During his visitation and funeral, I learned three lessons:

First, as I looked at the pictures of him that were displayed, I noticed what a truly warm and wonderful smile he had. I am not sure if I had ever noticed that before – it was just always there. When things are always there, it is far too easy to take them for granted. I vow to do a better job at appreciating the gifts that every person in my life has to offer.

Second, as all of us cousins gathered and we comforted each other over this loss, I had to wonder why we didn't find more time in our lives to see each other more often. Why do we meet only at funerals and weddings? I vow to make more time for that which is truly important in my life.

Third, as friend after friend and student after student and professor after professor came by the visitation to tell us how they knew Jimmy and what he meant to them, a clear pattern emerged about Jimmy: he always served others. Hearing what others had to say about Jimmy, I wondered: if this were my funeral, what would I want people to say about me? More importantly, am I living my life in such a way that it is in alignment with those words? I vow to do a better job at it.

Perhaps it's a cliché that in times of loss what's important becomes clear. Then it seems we forget these lessons as we return to the day to day. Yet these three lessons could have a transformational effect on our daily lives, and so I'm putting these in action:

1. Appreciate Others' Gifts
2. Connect with People
3. Live on Purpose

For Your Journal:

Appreciate Others' Gifts:

- *What are some gifts that people in your life offer?*
- *Would you like to appreciate those more versus taking them for granted? Why? If so, how will you do that?*

Connect with People:

- *How are you doing at regularly connecting with and seeing the important people in your life?*

- *What would happen if you connected more?*

- *If this is important to you, how will you start?*

Live on Purpose:

- *Are you satisfied with what people would say about you when you're gone? Why or why not?*

- *Of the contributions you have made so far, of what are you most proud?*

- *What are the contributions that you still must make?*

> *"Energy is the essence of life. Every day you decide how you're going to use it by knowing what you want and what it takes to reach that goal, and by maintaining focus."*
>
> Oprah Winfrey

You Are Always Saying No to Something

> "A man must be master of his hours and days, not their servant."
> William Frederick Book

As I went through the "travels" in the previous pages, I had developed a set of new priorities for my life. By now, hopefully you've done the same. But I had a problem. While the priorities were clear to me, so many other activities kept crowding in. As I've written before, we don't get results unless we put in the time and effort – but there's only so much time each day!

How do you protect your most important priorities and give yourself the time to work on them? In other words, how do you learn to say no to others and still feel okay with yourself? Like many people, I've had to work on saying "no" to some things so I could say "yes" to my priorities. This is an ongoing battle, especially when others are asking for our time and energy. Here are ten tools that can help you say "no":

1. Keep in mind that when you are saying "no" to something less vital, you are actually saying "yes" to those things that you have decided are a priority.

2. Remember that when someone asks you for time, it's a request. And, if the person making the request is being open and honest, then it is entirely reasonable to decline the request.

3. Since it is a request, you have every right to counter-offer. Here are a couple of ways to counter-offer:

> "I'd love to help out with that project; unfortunately, that deadline won't work with my schedule. Is the deadline flexible?"

> "I'd love to be part of that project; however, I'm not comfortable with the role that you are proposing for me. Could we discuss other ways that I might contribute?"

4. Instead of simply saying "no," is it possible to offer an alternative solution? For example, I allow myself two days a month where I will donate my time and do pro bono speaking events. It's not reasonable for me to do more than that (and maintain the rest of my schedule). Accordingly, if someone contacts me and wants me to speak at their monthly meeting for free and I'm already committed to my two dates that month, I simply say "Yes, I would be glad to. Unfortunately, that month doesn't work for me. Can we look at an alternative month?" In every case the answer has been yes.

5. Soften the "no" by giving something else. For example, "I'd love to come to your dinner party this weekend, however, I have really over committed this week, and so, regretfully, I'm going to say no. But I miss you – so can we chat on the phone next week?"

6. Understand that if you say "no" and the other person gets angry, it reflects a problem they're having. There is something else going on and you might want to probe to discover what that is (if it's important to you). Try this: "I can see that this is clearly important

to you. It seems that this goes a bit deeper than my saying no. Our relationship is important to me so I'd like to resolve this. Can we discuss it?"

7. Get all the information before committing. Don't say yes to anything until you fully understand what you are getting into. If you think it's something you are interested in say something like, "That sounds like something I'd like to be part of. However, before I make a decision, I'll need to know more about it." Things to learn (some of these apply more to business projects but are still good brainstorming examples):

> What – exactly – needs to be done?
>
> What is the deadline?
>
> How much time will it take?
>
> Will there be meetings? If so, in person or by phone?
>
> Who will I be working with?
>
> What results are we working towards?
>
> How will my performance be evaluated?

8. Know your priorities and be true to them. The reason that this helps us to say no gracefully is because then we are simply honoring a commitment that we have made to ourselves. If we don't know our own priorities, and we are constantly being swept along by others, we become resentful and that gets in the way of saying no with grace. Ask yourself this question: "How does this oppor-

tunity contribute to my priorities?"

9. If you find yourself always saying yes to others – as if you can't help yourself – have a standby line that forestalls the decision until you have time to think about it. Try this: "That sounds interesting and you know I'd love to help. Let me think about it and check my calendar and other commitments. I will get back to you by tomorrow."

10. Remember that it is, in fact, your choice. Perhaps the most profound choice of your life is how to spend it. Don't give up that power by saying "I can't say no" or "I have to." You always have choice (though some choices have unpleasant consequences). Hold onto that knowledge and practice exercising your personal power.

For Your Journal:

- *Do you know what it is that you want to say "yes" to?*
- *What is that?*
- *Why is it important to you?*
- *To what are you currently saying "yes" – but you don't really mean that (e.g., distractions)?*
- *Which of these could be eliminated or reduced TODAY? How?*
- *Which of the ten tips could you use, or what else could you use, to protect your boundaries and keep time for the most important priorities?*

Starting from the Top

"People often say that this or that person has not yet found himself. But the self is not something one finds, it is something one creates."

Thomas Szasz

professor of psychiatry, State University of New York (b. 1920)

I love Autumn! I love the change of the seasons. This past fall as I was out walking, enjoying the beautiful foliage, I noticed something: the majority of the trees seem to change colors starting at the top and working down. Likewise, they tend to lose their leaves starting at the top and working down.

I've thought about this as a metaphor for personal change: change happens at the top with our values and our purpose and works its way down into our daily choices, actions and behaviors. I don't mean that our values and our purpose will change with the seasons! Instead, what I mean is that for us to have truly deep, meaningful and lasting change in our lives, it has to begin with the pinnacle of our core values and purpose, then the changes must line up to support that. If our changes are not aligned with values and purpose, the changes will likely fail.

Too many times we try to make a change in our daily routine and it feels like punishment or like we are sacrificing something. However, when we can see how it is actually in line with something that is important to us, it is no longer a sacrifice. Here are a few examples:

Value: To be strong and healthy.

Implementation: I eat well and work out. When I'm in line with the value, I don't worry about dieting and sacrificing, I just enjoy being healthy.

Value: Authenticity.

Implementation: I strive for authentic, assertive, yet caring, communication. When I'm in line with the value, it guides me in my interactions; I don't feel afraid of being honest and asking questions and really listening for the answers.

Value: Developing Others

Implementation: I seek to help people understand how they can contribute, which helps me avoid judging.

To illustrate, I'll explain this last one in more detail: In school, when I have to work on team projects, I have often found myself extremely frustrated. Not that that will never happen again, however, several years ago, I started to really focus on drawing everyone into the project and giving them a space to contribute. While this has required work on my part, what I have found is that those who I, in the past, would have quickly written off as slackers (my bad assumption!), were actually happy to contribute. One woman told me at the end of our project that she'd never been on a team where the leader helped her understand how and where to contribute what she could.

This is something that can be challenging for me: I'm a straight-ahead, get-it-done type of person. However, a key value of mine is helping others believe in and expand their own potential. How can I do that if I simply charge ahead?

For Your Journal:

- *What are three of your values?*
- *For each value, how do you (or could you) implement that?*
- *What would be the benefit of each implementation?*

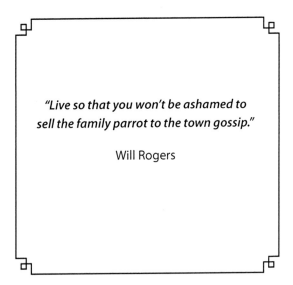

"Live so that you won't be ashamed to sell the family parrot to the town gossip."

Will Rogers

Success

"If your success is not on your terms, if it looks good to the world but doesn't feel good in your heart, it is not success at all."

Anna Quindlen

Starting when I was twelve, I picked and sold blackberries. One of my customers was Mr. Bushmeyer; he was about 80 years old and one of the most active people I had ever met. Instead of quietly sitting on his porch in a rocking chair, he rattled around his property in an old pick-up truck. He would load hay bales in the back and spread them around his 100 acres for his large herd of cattle. He took even more pleasure in his herd of grandchildren. He always had time to talk to me when I would deliver his blackberries. That was a treat for a young kid: an adult who took the time to talk and, more importantly, to listen. He always called me the Little Blackberry Girl.

About ten years ago, his health started declining and he had to move in with his family. The family fought over who would get to have him in their house. Their solution was that they would rotate every three months or so. They all wanted him nearby. I went to visit him at his granddaughter's house. I told her who I was and asked if I could visit with him. She graciously ushered me in, and as I walked into the room, Mr. Bushmeyer (who was then in his late 90s) cried out, "It's the Little Blackberry Girl!"

His granddaughter turned to me and said, "Now I know who you are! I've heard all about you. About what a good kid you were and what a hard worker you were and how you were always so nice to my grandfather." I sat and visited with the two of them for a long while.

As I was getting up to go, Mr. Bushmeyer took my hand and said, "You know, I've had a good life. I probably don't have much left, but I've loved every minute of what I've had. Do you want to know the secret of it?" Of course I did and told him so. He went on to tell me that as a young man he had heard a poem that moved him so much he committed it to memory and always kept it in front of him. He then recited that poem to me (from memory, in his late 90s!). Here it is:

Success

To laugh often and much,

To win the respect of intelligent people and the affection of children,

To earn the appreciation of honest critics and endure the betrayal of false friends,

To appreciate the beauty, to find the best in others!

To leave the world a bit better, whether by a healthy child,

a garden patch or a redeemed social condition,

to know even one life has breathed easier because you have lived.

This is to have succeeded.

Ralph Waldo Emerson

When he finished reciting the poem, I hugged him and told him that his life was a mirror of that poem. I am so thankful that he not only shared this poem with me but that he lived this poem and was a role model for me (even though I probably didn't know it at the time). What a successful man he was. He taught me to come up with my own definition of success and then craft a life to achieve it.

For Your Journal

- *How do you define success?*

- *Would others around you instantly recognize you in that definition?*

- *What's one commitment you'd like to make that will let your definition of success shine even more brightly in your daily life?*

Tapping Into Our Power

Conclusion

Paradoxically, perhaps, the greatest gift that we can give to others is to develop our own personal power. Why? Developing our personal power, growing so we are the source of our own power, leads to important results:

- We don't need to get power from others;

- We are free to give rather than take;

- We experience true freedom in that no matter what others do or say, they cannot take from us our desired future. Our future depends not on them, but on ourselves and our responses;

- We become inspiring examples for others;

- We lead without coercion;

- We give permission to those around us to create the life they want;

- We show up for others – just for them – without agendas, without attachments, without guilt, without resentment, without needing to control them (because when we're strong we don't need to play those games);

- Others recognize our travels and choose us as their guide;

- We experience true and deep happiness. This is where

the distinction between happiness and pleasure is so important. There are parts of the journey that are far from pleasant, but, if our ultimate destination is a fully self-empowered life, then those periods of unpleasantness are merely bumps on the road to someplace magnificent.

- We can help others in their development, and therefore, enrich their lives.

At the very heart of personal power is accepting choice. If we do not accept the fact that we are responsible for the choices we make – and that no one else gets to make those choices unless we let them – we will never change our thinking or our circumstances or our life.

Once a person claims and owns their personal power, she becomes the leader of her own life. There is no one end-point to this process, though; it is a life-long exploration. We don't know all the places we'll need to travel and we may wander down some dusty detours along the way. Yet with preparation, we can make meaning even from these detours.

Packing our bags for the travel is an important step for the adventure. To begin, let's pack our bags with some essentials, like awareness, personal responsibility, self-knowledge. Then let's add the ability to make choices that are in line with our values. On the adventure we need to find a sense of meaning, courage, and resiliency to add. Perhaps most importantly, we need a survival kit: a commitment to learn and grow. Then our travels can be rewarding, fun and meaningful.

These are great rewards, but there is one greater. By traveling our path with care and respect we can give others the inspiration and license to take their own travels toward leadership; perhaps in so doing, we become leaders ourselves. In other words, ***only by going on the journey for yourself can you earn the privilege of being a guide for others.***

About the Author

Bobbi is a leadership coach and educator for working managers, emerging leaders and everyday leaders. She is an expert at bringing the science of human performance into practical learning that people can use to achieve results and improve their lives.

Bobbi has been developing managers and building high-performing teams for more than 20 years for firms in financial services, professional services and technology industries. In addition to a background in managing people, she has studied individual and team performance for the last ten years and will complete her Masters degree in Positive Organizational Development and Change at Case Western Reserve in 2010. Bobbi speaks on leadership throughout the U.S.

In her free time, she loves to play disc golf with her husband, Rick. They live with their five cats in Chicago and Vail, Colorado. She can be reached at bobbi@bobbikahler.com. Learn more on her blog, Developing Your Inner Leader at www.bobbikahler.com.

About the Publisher

Travels of the Heart is published by Six Seconds - supporting people to create positive change by harnessing the power and wisdom of emotions.

Learn more about *Travels of the Heart* and other Six Seconds emotional intelligence publications online:

www.6seconds.org/tools